D0194925

Developing Superior Work Teams

Building Quality and the Competitive Edge

Dennis C. Kinlaw

Lexington Books
D.C. Heath and Company/Lexington, Massachusetts/Toronto

in association with

University Associates, Inc.
San Diego, California

Library of Congress Cataloging-in-Publication Data
Kinlaw, Dennis C.
Developing superior work teams : building quality and the
competitive edge / Dennis C. Kinlaw.
p.   cm.
"Published in association with University Associates."
Includes bibliographical references and index.
ISBN 0-669-24983-1
1. Work groups.   I. Title.
HD66.K56   1991
658.4'02—dc20   90-41348
                                                              CIP

Copyright © 1991 by Lexington Books

Published simultaneously in Canada
Printed in the United States of America
Casebound International Standard Book Number: 0-669-24983-1
Library of Congress Catalog Card Number: 90-41348

The paper used in this publication meets
the minimum requirements of American National Standard
for Information Sciences—Permanence of Paper
for Printed Library Materials, ANSI Z39.48-1984.

Year and number of this printing:

92 93 94   8 7 6 5 4 3

*This book is dedicated
to my many friends and colleagues in NASA,
and its contractors
through whom I have learned most of what I
know
about teams and teamwork.*

Contents

Figures

Preface

Two realities are shaping organizational life in America today. The first reality is that all organizations are faced with the same primary challenge: they will either produce consistently superior services and products, or they will soon not be producing much at all. The second reality is that superior teamwork and developing superior work teams have been demonstrated to be the only consistent strategies for producing superior services and products.

The evidence is now quite unequivocal. Teams and teamwork make the competitive difference.

The purpose of this book is to provide managers and other key people (like trainers and consultants) with the practical tools that they require for building superior teamwork and developing superior work teams. The specific assistance that the reader can expect to find in this book includes:

- a clear picture of just what teamwork and work teams are;

- a model of the primary characteristics of superior work teams;

- many practical guidelines and suggestions for developing superior work teams;

- a set of powerful Key Strategies for developing superior work teams; and

- a description of the kinds of skills that leaders of superior work teams must have.

All the concepts in this book have been derived from experience in the workplace. To be sure, many are supported and corroborated by other authors. But I did not begin my investigation of teams and teamwork in the library. I began seriously thinking about teams and teamwork when I found myself in the midst of trying to help organizations build teams and foster teamwork in the face of enormous obstacles and in extraordinarily complex environments.

Over the past several years the major focus of my consulting work has been on building superior work teams. Because teamwork and the development of work teams are so integral to Total Quality Management, much of my work has naturally been in assisting organizations in their Total Quality Management initiatives.

I have analyzed work groups in a variety of ways and tried to discover how work groups are different from work teams. But above all, I have tried to discover what distinguishes *superior* work teams from other work teams and work units.

My experience in analyzing work groups and teams has included many intense team-building interventions that involved individual work groups as well as interface groups from multiple proprietary companies. Much of my time in the recent past has been spent in helping NASA's Kennedy Space Center respond to a multitude of challenges to team performance brought on, first, by massive contractual and organizational changes that took place shortly before the *Challenger* accident, and, second, by problems in team breakups and performance caused by the accident itself.

Just as the concepts in this book have been primarily derived from my personal experience in the workplace, they have also been proven in the workplace. The reader can approach the material in this book confident that it is grounded in the real world of work and certain that the ideas, models, tools, and techniques presented here can make a demonstrable difference in the total performance of work teams.

This book reflects my conviction that the number-one priority of organizations should be to change every work unit into a superior work team and to make superior teamwork the norm for organizational behavior. This priority requires that all the leaders and other key people in our organizations have the practical knowledge and tools to be builders of superior teamwork and superior work teams. I have written this book to provide them with that knowledge and at least some of those tools.

Introduction

Teamwork is surely one of the most admired and praised characteristics of organizations. It is an ideal that managers and employees revere with something approaching religious fervor. In the many years that I have consulted with organizations, I have heard all sorts of complaints from all kinds of jobholders. But there is one complaint I have never heard—people have never said to me that there was too much teamwork in their organization.

The chief executive of a major aerospace group regularly reminds his subalterns that teamwork is one of his "gold watches." And his executive staff knows that "you just don't drop a gold watch."

When NASA successfully returned to manned space flight and launched the first shuttle since the tragic *Challenger* accident, the center director of NASA's Kennedy Space Center sent out a congratulatory letter to every employee at the center. The primary characteristic of the return-to-flight process that he chose to emphasize—above all else—was teamwork. The letter read (emphases mine):

Dear Fellow *Team Member:*

When the U.S. orbiter *Discovery* lifted off on the ST-26 mission to return the United States to manned space flight, there were ... unusual items of "cargo" in the mid-deck area. One was a very special book, signed by virtually everyone at KSC, expressing the support of the KSC *team* "from liftoff to landing."

Managers routinely appeal to a group's *team spirit* when dissensions and conflict erupt; they urge their people to *pull together*

when the group faces major challenges; and they predictably con-
gratulate the whole *team* when difficult milestones and production
goals are met.

The word *team* finds its way easily into organizations' logos
and rallying cries. *Team Excellence* is the current motto of a major
NASA installation. *Team Report* is the title of the newsletter of a
Florida-based engineering firm. *Go Team* is emblazoned on the T-
shirts of a software project team.

In a *Harvard Business Review* article, Reich (1987) maintains
that the American myth of the entrepreneur, as depicted in books
such as Horatio Alger's *Ragged Dick,* is the enemy of economic
revival and that our real hope lies in teamwork and the team.

> To the extent that we continue to celebrate the traditional myth
> of the entrepreneurial hero, we will slow the progress of change
> and adaptation that is essential to our economic success. If we are
> to compete effectively in today's work, we must begin to celebrate
> collective entrepreneurship, endeavors in which the whole of the
> effort is greater than the sum of individual contributions. We need
> to honor our teams more, our aggressive leaders and maverick
> geniuses less.

McDonnell Douglas recently underwent a major reorganization
and reassignment of all its managers and supervisors (McDonnell
Douglas 1989). All managers and supervisors had to compete for
their jobs based on their subordinates', peers', and superiors' perceptions of their abilities to lead. The first characteristic evaluated
was: "Teamplayer: Unites others toward a shared destiny through
sharing information and ideas, empowering others and developing
trust."

There is no reason to doubt that managers have a strong and
genuine belief in team performance. This belief is daily reinforced
as more and more organizations begin to recognize that whatever
they do or produce today is not good enough for tomorrow.

Wherever we go in organizations today we see prominently displayed posters emblazoned with such slogans as *Quality Team.* One
very popular poster issued by the Association for Quality Control
reads, "Quality—The Result of Teamwork."

Total Quality Management and Teamwork

A recent general programmatic initiative that has drawn greater attention to teamwork as the key to organizational success is Total Quality Management (TQM). These programs consistently emphasize various strategies such as focus on the customer, continuous improvement, total employee involvement, and the like. Their emphases may vary somewhat from organization to organization. But there is one emphasis that we find in all TQM programs without exception. It is teamwork.

William Scherkenbach (1988) describes W. Edwards Deming's fourteen points for achieving quality as a "customer-driven, team-fueled . . . approach." Florida Power and Light (FPL) is the first (and only) American company to receive the prestigious Deming Award for quality. FPL's TQM program is clearly team centered. Through the strategy of team formation and development, FPL has renewed its internal communication networks and strengthened its relationships with customers and suppliers.

Just how integral team development and teamwork are to TQM is apparent in such companies as Martin Marietta's Space Launch Systems Company (*Aviation Week and Space Technology* 1988). The company's TQM plan calls for some fourteen thousand employees to be trained in a three-day program that stresses teamwork. Following the training program employees are organized into high performance teams and management teams. Vice President for Production John R. Adamoli and his staff function as a high-performance leadership and steering team.

As teams mature at Martin Marietta, they are expected to assume more and more responsibilities for the management of themselves and for every aspect of their work life, such as setting their work and vacation schedules and establishing team performance goals and budgets. Some teams are responsible for totally redesigning work process systems, such as the Titan rocket factory assembly floor.

With Martin's increased emphasis on teamwork, rewards are increasingly focused on team performance. Rewards are structured to return a percentage of increases in the "bottom line" to teams that are responsible for achieving their own performance goals, while using their own improvement strategies and techniques.

Douglas Aircraft emphasizes teams in the TQM commitment statement that every employee is expected to sign. Employees commit to the vision that "quality is the supreme value" and to specific responsibilities "to cooperate with all their *teammates* [emphasis mine] in this new way of working together to build airplanes" (Holpp 1989).

Work Teams and the Changing Roles
of Managers and Supervisors

The emphasis on teamwork and developing work teams is having far-reaching implications for changes in the traditional roles of managers and supervisors. M&M/Mars has opened a new plant in Waco, Texas, with self-managed teams. TRW has a plant in Lawrence, Kansas, in which supervision has been eliminated. At Ibis, producer of industrial enzymes, teams are largely autonomous. At Aetna Life, self-managed teams take care of all the functions for processing claims. These teams are responsible for the traditional supervisory functions of hiring, work scheduling, overtime, and performance evaluations (Sherwood 1988). The Johnsonville Sausage Company has eliminated supervisors and organized its production around pride teams, which are responsible for managing themselves (Peters 1985).

Twenty percent of General Electric's work force of 120,000 employees has been organized into self-managing work teams. The corporate goal is to have 35 percent of its work force organized into self-managing teams. GE expects to realize a 40- to 50-percent improvement in productivity by organizing its work force into teams (Business Week 1989).

The many radical and far-reaching changes in the way organizations are being restructured into self-managed teams has dramatic implications for the roles and functions of managers and supervisors. Where the jobs of managers and supervisors are surviving, we can observe a shift

- from managing by control to managing by commitment;

- from focusing on individual motivation and output to focusing on team motivation and output; and

- from the traditional functions of planning, organizing, staffing, evaluating to the functions of coaching and facilitating.

Total Quality Management initiatives have increased organizations' emphasis on and commitment to teamwork and team development by orders of magnitude. Teamwork has been demonstrated to be the single consistent strategy for continuous improvement in quality and for increased competitiveness. The movement toward teamwork has taken on the proportions of an avalanche roaring through American firms and sweeping most traditional resistances before it. Traditional distinctions between supervisors and employees, management, and labor are being swept away, but where these distinctions still remain, they account for most shortfalls in the performance of organizations.

The challenges that organizations face to remain competitive are enormous. The competitive game is tough, and it will—without question—get tougher. The organizations that are winning are those that are using team development and teamwork to make the leaps in innovation, quality, and efficiency that they must make— if they are to survive.

The key position that teamwork has in performance is captured in the criteria that the National Aeronautics and Space Administration uses to award its prestigious NASA Excellence Award. One criterion that companies competing for the award must meet is that their employees must be trained to participate "in building . . . teamwork" (NASA 1989).

There is, then, a growing commitment to team development and teamwork by managers—stimulated to a large degree by TQM initiatives. Team development is being increasingly accepted as the key to regaining and keeping the quality and competitive edge. In superior teams the synergistic effect is apparent. One plus one plus one equals a lot more than three.

The closer-knit a group becomes, the greater the dynamism it creates. The greater the commitment within a group to a set of common goals, the greater the likelihood that members of the group will make personal sacrifices to meet these goals.

The Need for a Practical Model

Teamwork is what leverages the potential of an organization into superior results. Teamwork is the vehicle for integrating information, technology, competence, and resources—starting with the human. Teamwork is the fundamental requisite for continuous improvement. It can leverage the potential of any organization to unimagined levels of sustained superior performance and continuous improvement.

But although there is a present and growing commitment to developing teams and fostering teamwork on the part of managers and other key employees, their level of commitment is rarely matched by the practical knowledge and skills for turning work groups and total organizations into superior teams.

Team development is not easy, and it is not simple. Even under the best of conditions, it can be a task of mind-boggling, back-breaking difficulty. But without a clear, functional model to guide us, the task becomes so confused and contaminated with unsupported opinion and bias that it is impossible. Consider a recent experience.

A year or so ago, I was asked to design and implement a team development program for a large architectural firm. After I made a preliminary analysis of the firm's readiness to begin a team development initiative, I cataloged the following five conditions that were working against team development in this firm.

1. Each of the major organizational elements in the firm was set up to bill the others for internal services, and the result was an enormous amount of internal competitiveness, bickering over chargeable costs and distrust.

2. The firm had doubled in size in each of five successive years and undergone numerous organizational changes. Whatever informal network had existed at one time was now badly damaged and not working.

3. In the process of rapid growth, new professionals had been hired at better rates than many of those who had been with the firm since it started. A lot of resentment built among the older hands toward the new hires.

4. The firm had no strategic plan, and people had little sense of long-term direction. Work groups and individuals had very disparate perceptions of what was important and what was not.

5. The founder still ran the organization and had developed an inner ring of confidants who operated from Mount Olympus and who had no interest in sharing their visions and power with the mere mortals who occupied the lesser heights.

But the biggest impediment of all to initiating a team development process in this firm was that none of its decision makers had a functional picture of what team development was all about. As a result, I was unable to develop a consensus about such a picture or model, and I finally abandoned the project.

Over the past several years I have become deeply involved in understanding and improving work-team development and performance. Much of my work has been in conjunction with assisting organizations in their TQM initiatives. I have analyzed work groups in a variety of ways and tried to discover the general functional characteristics of work groups that distinguish them from work teams. But above all, I have tried to discover what distinguishes superior work teams from other work teams.

The data that I have compiled from these many team-focused activities and interventions have led me to the following three conclusions:

1. Managers and employees have experiences on work teams— especially superior work teams—that they describe as remarkably similar.

2. Managers and employees rarely have an explicit model of team development and performance that describes clearly the functional characteristics of superior teams.

3. Managers and employees, largely because they have no well-defined model, often cannot efficiently initiate a set of integrated strategies for developing teams capable of sustained superior performance.

Questions and Answers

In order to build and maintain superior teams (both temporary teams, as in projects, and permanent teams, as in work groups), managers and other key players must have a model or picture of what superior teams are like. I have tried to build a model of team development and performance that answers the following questions: (1) What do superior work teams achieve, and how do their results differ from the results of other groups and teams? (2) What are the critical processes in team performance that lead to superior performance? (3) What do members of superior teams feel that distinguishes them from other groups and teams? and (4) What are the characteristics of leadership in superior teams that distinguish it from traditional leadership in work groups?

My sources for creating a model of superior team development and performance have been:

- interviews with over two hundred work-team members and leaders;

- data obtained from over three thousand people from ten different organizations attending a two-day team-development seminar associated with implementing an integrated TQM program;

- data obtained from several hundred managers attending my two-day seminar, "Practical Team Development for Managers"; and

- a review of studies published over the past twenty years on work groups and work teams.

Later chapters in this book are devoted to describing in considerable length the superior work-team development and performance model that has resulted from my studies. The model is used as the basis for describing the key leverage points on which team leaders and other key organizational people should concentrate to maximize their efforts to build superior work teams.

Purposes and Objectives of This Book

The purpose of this book is to provide managers and other key people (like trainers and consultants) with a functional model that they can use for developing superior work teams. The book is particularly useful in undertaking the team development process that is so critical in TQM initiatives. The book has been designed for use in several ways:

- as a self-help guide for leaders to make their work groups into superior work teams;

- as a conceptual basis for trainers to use to equip others to build superior work teams;

- as an adjunct resource for participants involved in any team-development program; and

- as a special guide for people having responsibilities in TQM team-development initiatives.

The specific objectives of the book are, first, to present the Model for Superior Team Development and Performance and clarify each of its elements, and, second, to describe a set of Key Strategies that can be used to address the key elements in the model and move teams toward superior development and performance.

Organization of the Book

This book is built on my own work and studies. But it also reflects and tries to take into account the studies published by others about work teams and related topics.

Because I have intended that this book—above all else—be used and applied to the task of team development, I have kept to a minimum the use of references in the text proper. In the "References and Resources" section, however, is a list of those studies referred to in the text, as well as other relevant resources.

Chapters and Content

The chapters that follow are previewed below.

Chapter 1: Groups, Teams, and Superior Teams

Groups differ from teams, and both differ from superior work teams in a number of ways. This chapter prepares the reader for understanding and using the superior-work-team development and performance model by defining the functional differences between groups, teams, and superior teams.

Chapter 2: Team Building and Team Development— What's the Difference?

Team building and team development are not the same thing, even though the terms are normally used interchangeably and careful distinctions are not typically made between them. This chapter suggests that there are quite important distinctions that must be made that have a functional significance for developing and maintaining superior work teams.

Chapter 3: Overview of the Model for Superior Team Development and Performance

The characteristics that distinguish a superior work team from all other kinds of work groups fall into four categories: Results, Informal Processes, Feelings, and Leadership. This chapter gives a rationale for making these characteristics the practical basis for understanding and building superior work teams.

Chapter 4: Focusing on Results

The critical practical difference between superior work teams and all other work units becomes most apparent when we compare the results that superior work teams produce with the results of other work units. They produce superior results. This chapter explores in detail these results and describes their implications for superior-work-team development and performance.

Chapter 5: Focusing on Informal Team Processes

Superior work teams use a number of effective and efficient processes for achieving superior results. These processes include communicating and contacting, responding and adapting, influencing and improving, and appreciating and celebrating. These processes are discussed and their implications drawn for superior-work-team development and performance.

Chapter 6: Focusing on Team Feelings

Members of superior work teams describe how they feel as team members in distinctive and consistent terms. Certain kinds of team norms and actions are conducive to the emergence and growth of these feelings, and certain kinds are not. This chapter describes these important feelings and how they are nurtured.

Chapter 7: Focusing on Team Leadership

Most superior work teams develop and continue because of the kinds of leaders that they have. Leadership roles and functions in superior teams are very different from the traditional roles and functions of managers, supervisors, and other work-unit leaders. This chapter draws some fundamental distinctions between traditional leadership and superior team leadership, and it describes the roles, functions, and behaviors required of superior leaders.

Chapter 8: Key Strategies for Superior-Work-Team Development and Performance

This chapter describes in detail several Key Strategies for improving the four primary elements in the Model for Superior Team Development and Performance. The strategies have been selected for their comprehensiveness and their multiple impact on superior-work-team development and performance.

Conclusion

This section of the book briefly reviews the key points and makes some final observations of what real-life superior teams are like.

Appendix: Tools for Team Development and Performance

This appendix contains a copy of the Team Development Questionnaire and a couple of rational problem-solving tools.

References and Recommended Additional Reading

Although references have been kept to a minimum throughout the book, I have wanted to ensure that all material that relates to the work of others was properly acknowledged. These sections include bibliographical information on citations made in the text as well as a number of sources that have either historical or practical value.

1
Groups, Teams, and Superior Teams

This book is about superior work teams, and its purpose is to equip managers and other key organizational players (like trainers and consultants) with the necessary understanding and skills to build them. My expectation is that people involved in special initiatives—like Total Quality Management—intended to improve total organizations through improved work teams will find this book especially helpful.

In order to delimit my topic precisely, I should like at the very outset to define what I mean by **superior work teams** and **team development.** In this chapter I will define superior work teams; in the next chapter I will describe team development and highlight important differences between team development and team building.

There are no commonly accepted definitions of *group, teamwork,* or *team* (Wagner et al. 1977). But some commonsense definitions can be developed that are based on observation and experience and that, above all, are functional—that is, they can be used to guide the actions of managers and others interested in developing superior teams. Four terms require definition: *teamwork, work group, work team,* and *superior work team.*

Teamwork

Teamwork is a condition that may come and go. It may exist only for the time that it takes a group to perform a particular task; after the task is performed, the need for teamwork no longer exists. Group members can have teamwork one moment, then be disjunctive and at odds with each other the next. People can rally around some purpose and cooperate to achieve it, then break up and become very competitive and proprietary.

Teamwork can exist in at least the following kinds of work units:

- *Management groups.* These are major decision-making groups such as CEOs and senior executives, executive boards, or corporate planning groups.

- *Permanent work groups.* These are groups of people who work more or less daily with each other and who have a specific organizational name. They may be branches, sections, or long-term-project groups.

- *Temporary or special-purpose groups.* These are groups of people who have joined together to perform a specific task. They usually represent a variety of organizational elements. Examples are quality circles, special-project teams, performance improvement teams, accident-investigation teams, tiger teams, horizontal teams, vertical teams, cross-functional teams, and standing committees.

- *Interface groups.* These are groups made up of two or more units from different organizations that have a permanent work relationship and that must cooperate to get their jobs done. Examples are interfaces between users and suppliers; design, manufacturing, and marketing; operations and maintenance; electrical and mechanical subsystems; procurement and users; and training and users.

- *Networks.* These are groups of people who may not have face-to-face contact, but who depend on each other for information, for expert advice, for alerts, and for "heads-up" about changes and problems. Examples are networks among secretaries, networks among corporate and field people, networks among experts and professionals, and networks among users and contractors.

Teamwork can exist in any of these settings, to a very small degree or to a very pronounced degree. Teamwork does not necessarily describe a permanent condition. In fact, it becomes a permanent condition only in superior work teams.

Teamwork's most commonsense meaning is the functional and qualitative aspects of what work units do when they act like a team.

The **qualitative** meaning of the term is apparent in such everyday expressions as "We worked closely together," "We always helped each other," "We were all focused on a common goal," "It was a team effort, everyone contributed," and the like. Qualitatively, *teamwork* describes the functioning of a group of people who are closely knit around a common purpose, who work easily together, and who have positive work relationships.

The **functional** meaning of teamwork is the ways people must work together and cooperate in order to produce some product or service that cannot be produced by a single person.

Theoretically, teamwork can exist anywhere for any period of time. It can exist in families, in school classes, among manufacturers and their clients, between marketing and production—even between management and labor. It is clearly to our collective advantage to help teamwork exist all the time in all social groups—at work as well as at church, school, and home.

The various subdivisions within organizations too often exist as multiple fiefdoms, loosely tied federations, or out-and-out enemies. Most organizations have an unlimited opportunity for increasing or enhancing teamwork—and it is certainly to their competitive advantage to do so.

The Japanese recognized this advantage back in the 1950s. Japanese strategies for new product development and quality assurance are built solidly upon a commitment to team development across all departments. There is the tightest association between marketing, design, manufacturing, inspection, and sales. All these organizational units are fully represented at each step (and at each iteration of each step) of the new product development cycle of plan–do–check–act.

The Japanese also recognize the critical value of extending teamwork beyond parent organizations to include suppliers or vendors. Japanese teamwork strategy rests upon the obvious fact that the quality of complex modern products depends totally on the quality of their component parts. The level of quality required by manufacturers of components they purchase cannot be assured through inspection at the point of acquisition.

It is clearly to a manufacturer's advantage that components meet the criterion "fit to use" 100 percent of the time. Japanese manufacturers have solved the problem of quality components by teamwork—by establishing and maintaining cooperation, open communication, and trust with their suppliers.

The way the Japanese manufacturers go about fostering teamwork with their suppliers is instructive. They do three very important things:

1. They distribute to potential suppliers a list of criteria that will be used in their selection. Most often the suppliers have input into these criteria.

2. They make positive guidance and quality control training freely available to their suppliers to help them succeed.

3. They include representatives from the manufacturing company, by invitation of the suppliers, in the suppliers' internal quality-control audits.

The extraordinary results that teamwork is achieving in Japan can be illustrated in a single example. Twenty years ago, Japanese television manufacturers requested that their suppliers set a goal in their defect rate of ten per million. Through teamwork between manufacturers and their suppliers, the goal was met (Kondo 1988).

The level of teamwork between buyer and supplier in Japan is perhaps best illustrated by a remarkable document published in 1969. In that year, manufacturing companies and their vendors collaborated to issue "Ten Vendee-Vendor Relations from the Standpoint of Quality Control." This document is now considered the norm for negotiating vendee-vendor contracts in Japan.

AT&T Network Systems has learned what the Japanese expect from its vendee-vendor team. Its contract with Nippon Telegraph and Telephone (NTT) does not allow AT&T to replace or upgrade bad units or submit failure reports that say "no trouble was found."

This NTT requirement had an effect not only on AT&T not only but on all AT&T vendors. AT&T and its own vendor team, in their analysis of each defective unit returned to them, must identify the root cause of failure and the corrective action that will prevent the problem from occurring again. In this and similar cases, teamwork between user and supplier produced a win-win outcome for everyone. All parties become more competitive by uncovering ways to improve the quality of their designs and manufacturing.

Fortunately, the United States can also boast some good examples of teamwork across internal and external organizational boundaries. Digital Equipment Company (DEC) has an enviable record in supplying quality replacement parts to its customers. At DEC, spare parts are called field replaceable units (FRUs). To insure total customer satisfaction, DEC created a field service logistics quality-assurance group made up of people from marketing, engineering, manufacturing, logistics, and field service.

At NASA's Kennedy Space Center, all support services are supplied by a single contractor—EG&G Florida. The EG&G Florida contract is monitored by members of Kennedy's Institution Support Directorate. Managers from NASA and from EG&G Florida now develop a common strategic plan to insure that they pursue common goals, have clearly agreed-on priorities, and are able to work in an environment of mutual trust.

Motorola recently won the highly prized U.S. award for quality, the Malcolm Baldrige National Quality Award. Motorala has traditionally had a very close relationship with its suppliers and meets with them regularly as a group to exchange information. Recently, Motorola reemphasized this relationship in conjunction with requiring its suppliers to compete for the Baldrige Award. Motorola offers free to its suppliers its own specially developed courses on design manufacturability, assembly, statistical process control, and cycle time management (*Techknowledge* 1989).

The Oilwell Cable Division of TRW was opened in the late 1970s in Lawrence, Kansas. The primary organizational emphasis of TRW was teamwork. Its goal was to make work groups themselves the lowest level of management. Since 1978, the company has reported an 80 percent annual increase in productivity.

A "teaming" effort between the civil service and contractor at

NASA's Ames Research Center, produced a remote oil skimmer system that resulted in a reduction in the amount of hazardous waste removed from machine shops and an annual savings of $6,000 a year (NASA 1989).

An engineering firm in Texas has organized a Human Resources Team composed of representatives from all the subdivisions of the organization. The team identifies employees' short- and long-term concerns. It investigates, resolves, and closes out the short-term concerns, and it develops and proposes systemic changes to upper management for resolving the long-term ones.

One consultant working with a basic manufacturing plant in Omaha reports helping management and the company's union, the International Brotherhood of Electrical Workers, build a new culture of teamwork. The result was an increase in productivity of 52 percent over eighteen months (Miller 1984).

Teamwork can exist anywhere within an organization and anywhere between organizations. It includes a multitude of processes that have a single purpose—to transcend the limits of individual jobholders or individual organizational units and achieve more than it is possible for individuals or separate work units to achieve.

Teamwork is not an entity, like a work group, work team, or superior work team. Rather, it describes certain qualities or functions that may exist in a group for a period of time. In work groups, teamwork may exist not at all or only sporadically. In work teams, teamwork exists most of the time. In superior work teams, teamwork is intense and persistent and exists all the time as a way of life.

In summary, then, I use *teamwork* throughout this book to describe:

- a highly desirable condition that can exist for any period of time—long or short—in any group;

- the *qualitative* characteristics of groups, like being closely knit together around a common purpose, working easily together, and having positive work relationships;

- the *functional* characteristics of units that must work together and cooperate in order to produce a product or service that cannot be produced by a single person; and

- the multitude of actions, processes, feelings, and results that distinguish work groups from work teams and work teams from superior work teams.

The main portion of this book elaborates the meaning of *teamwork* and provides guidance for achieving teamwork to the marked degree that it exists in superior work teams.

The next steps in creating a concrete and functional description of teamwork will be:

1. to develop a definition of *work group;*

2. to discuss the important characteristics of *work teams;*

3. to clarify further some basic *differences between work groups and work teams;* and

4. to describe the distinguishing characteristics of *superior work teams.*

Much information has been published about work groups and a good bit has been published about work teams, but very little has been written about superior work teams. (Recent examples are Nieva et al. 1985 and Hackman 1983.) Work groups, work teams, and superior work teams share some characteristics. But the farther we move from work groups toward superior work teams, the more these similarities disappear and the more the distinctive characteristics of superior teams emerge.

Work Groups

A *work group* is a set of two or more jobholders who make up some identifiable organizational unit that is considered to be a permanent part of an organization—like a section, branch, or office. Work groups are the basic building blocks of organizational performance. These are the units where the work of individuals comes together to form services and products that are conveyed to a user either within or without the organization.

Typically, work groups have a single supervisor or lead. They usually do not exceed thirty employees. Work groups may exceed thirty employees and use various forms of leadership, but what is distinctive about work groups is not the number of their members or their form of leadership. What is distinctive about them is that they exist to perform a set of tasks that, in some way, contributes to make a larger whole. In other words, work groups cannot be defined quantitatively by the number of their members or leaders. They can best be described functionally by what they produce.

Work groups are the lowest level in an organization at which an additive or integrative process occurs. They are the operational demarcation in the processes of production at which individual performance is no longer the primary determinant of success.

In a wind-tunnel test group, for example, many individual players perform many separate and distinct tasks. There are sensor technicians, model fabricators, statisticians, and engineers, to name only a few. Each person in the group has a number of individual tasks that he or she performs completely alone. What marks the group as a group, however, is that all the tasks are subordinated to the final product of the group, which in this case is a technical report or research paper. All individual tasks, through processes of addition and integration, come together in a group product.

An automobile production line requires that thousands of separate tasks be completed by individual workers. At various points these individual tasks become part of a larger unit of production, such as the engine, chassis, drive chain and body. There are within the production line a variety of distinguishable work groups. These units mark the points at which individual performance becomes integrated into a larger unit of production.

The tasks of individuals in groups may be combined through processes that are additive, integrative, or interactive (figure 1-1). Various combinations of these three processes can, of course, also occur.

In **additive processes,** workers in the same group all use the same equipment or machine (such as a stamp press or lathe) to produce the same product, such as backing plates, winch cheeks, and cotter pins. The group's output is not integrated into a larger whole. Individual outputs are simply added together, and the sum becomes the group's output.

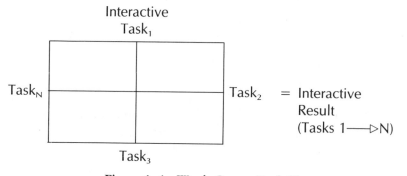

Additive

$$Task_1 + Task_2 + Task_3 + \ldots Task_N \qquad = Summary\ Result$$
$$(Tasks\ 1 \ldots N)$$

Integrative

$$Task_1 \longrightarrow Task_2 \longrightarrow Task_3 \ldots Task_N \qquad = Integrative\ Result$$
$$(Tasks\ 1 \longrightarrow N)$$

Interactive
$Task_1$

$Task_N$ $Task_2$ = Interactive
Result
$(Tasks\ 1 \longrightarrow N)$

$Task_3$

Figure 1–1. *Work Group Task Flows*

Production-line groups typically use **integrative processes.** What is placed on a chassis of a vehicle at an early stage in the production flow is not simply added but is integrated into a developing whole, in which all the parts are mutually interdependent.

In the case of design groups, software groups, budget groups, procurement groups, maintenance groups, and the like, the end service or product does not result simply by adding together what each individual does. Nor does their result occur through a process of linear (that is, one-way) integration. The process is, rather, **interactive.** There is a two-way flow of information and action between individuals by which the end product or service is produced.

The wind-tunnel test group referred to earlier also represents an example of interactive process. At various points, from conceiving a test to producing a technical report, the work of the test engineers, the model builders, and the statisticians must all come together in a way that is not simply additive or integrative. The end product—the technical report—is produced by hundreds of steps that require interaction between two or more individuals.

A work group that uses additive processes alone to produce a product or service may function without teamwork. Integrative and interactive processes, by their very nature, force at least minimal levels of cooperation or teamwork. But although work groups whose function involves integrative or interactive processes may have some degree of teamwork, they may not have the special characteristics of a *team*, as I will be using that term throughout this book.

Work groups, then, are units of two or more jobholders

- that typically do not exceed thirty people;

- whose leadership role is usually filled by one person;

- in which the work of individual group members is performed through processes that are additive, integrative, or interactive;

  and

- that are the primary unit of productivity in the organization.

In this book, I will use *work group* as a generic term to describe all work units that have this set of characteristics. Work teams and superior work teams share all the basic characteristics of work groups, but these primary units of performance do things that work groups do not do—that is, they are *functionally* different from work groups. They also do things better than work groups—that is, they are *qualitatively* different.

How Work Teams Differ from Work Groups

Even a cursory review of studies about work groups and work teams leads to at least two significant conclusions. First, these studies rarely make careful distinctions between groups and teams; and second, they often suggest that factors outside a group's control determine its ability to develop and function as a team.

The first point will be taken up later in this book. It is the second point that I should like to discuss now in order to clear up a fundamental misunderstanding about how teams are created.

Among the most common group factors studied that impact on a group's performance are (Nieva et al. 1985).

- the kinds of tasks performed
- group size
- cohesiveness
- organizational environment
- communication patterns, and
- homogeneity and heterogeneity among group members.

This list is by no means complete, but it is sufficient to highlight an unfortunate bias that has dominated research on work groups and work teams: the notion that external or objective factors largely determine a group's performance and (implicitly) its ability to develop into a team.

A brief look at the matter of group tasks will illustrate this point. Some writers hold that certain kinds of tasks require teamwork and other kinds do not. These writers conclude that the kinds of tasks workers perform will therefore determine whether they will develop into teams. A team, then, is a function of the kinds of tasks that a group does.

Davis (1969) suggests that when a group's tasks are unitary and not divisible, it is more likely that the group will function as a set of individuals and not develop into a team. Steiner (1972) suggests that team performance emerges only when tasks cease to be disjunctive and become conjunctive or additive. Disjunctive tasks are performed independently by group members and reflect individual choices among alternatives. Conjunctive tasks are performed together. Additive tasks require that individual tasks be collected into larger wholes.

Briggs and Johnston (1967) indicate that teams are characterized by the performance of interdependent tasks. They distinguished sequential and reciprocal tasks, with reciprocal requiring the higher level of coordination.

This notion that the kind of task performed influences or even determines group performance and team development has been carried over into current research (Hackman and Morris 1975; Hackman and Oldham 1980).

Clearly the more complex the tasks are, and the more conjunctive and additive they are, the more likely it is that group members must cooperate to perform the task and the more they must behave like teams. Certain kinds of tasks do lead inevitably to some level of team development. I have suggested that tasks that are performed by simple additive processes do not require teamwork, but tasks that require integrative or interactive processes do require teamwork, at least at a minimal level (figure 1–1).

But the kinds of tasks themselves are insufficient to inhibit the development of a work group into a work team. My position is that *every work group can become a work team and every work team can become a superior work team.* That individuals perform separate and uncoordinated tasks does not prohibit them from working together to accomplish a whole host of integrated functions that are characteristic of team behavior.

Even if the work performed by work-group members is not integrative or interactive, it is still possible and clearly more productive for members to

- share their ideas, to improve all the jobs and all the work processes in the group—whether the job or the process is theirs or not;

- develop coordinated responses to organizational changes that affect the whole group;

- build respect in their mutual relationships;

- participate in setting common improvement goals; and

- initiate common actions to show appreciation to colleagues for their superior performance.

The point that I am making is that work-team development is not finally prejudiced by the kinds of tasks that work groups perform. The nature of a group's tasks is quite secondary to the decision to become a team.

Groups may or may not decide to use processes that help them develop into teams. Processes like sharing information, mutual problem solving, giving support, committing to total customer satisfaction, and planning for continuous improvement can emerge in any group. And when these processes begin to emerge, the group is on the way to becoming a team.

Work Teams

Work teams are first of all work groups, but they are very much more than that. They are work groups that

- have reached a new plateau of productivity and quality;
- have developed (at least to a recognizable level) certain feelings among group members;
- have created certain critical work processes; and
- enjoy a special kind of leadership that acts through teamwork and focuses on both development and performance.

The differences between work groups and work teams can be described only superficially if we focus on tasks, size, or other such criteria. The main differences between groups and teams are qualitative and functional.

The functional difference becomes apparent because work teams do things that work groups don't do. Members of work teams not only cooperate in all aspects of their task performance, they share in what are traditionally thought of as management functions and responsibilities, such as joint planning, organizing the team, setting performance goals, assessing the team's performance, developing their own strategies to manage change, and securing their own resources.

The qualitative difference is apparent because even when work teams do what work groups do, they add value. Sharing of information is easier, issues are aired openly, and conflicts are resolved quickly and with positive results.

Consider the following contrasts. Work Group A and Work Group B both perform the same task—say, home phone installation. Both groups have members with the same levels of competency. Work Group A consistently outperforms Work Group B. What accounts for the difference in performance?

Work Group A does such things as:

- employing a variety of informal, spontaneous ways of recognizing the contributions that members make—doing the dirty jobs, keeping a cool head in crises, or trying to help members who are less experienced;

- holding a variety of informal social get-togethers to help members develop friendly and personal relationships; and

- meeting regularly to keep everyone informed about changes in policy, work load, work equipment, personnel, and so on.

In Work Group A it is easy for members to make suggestions to improve the quality and efficiency of their jobs. There is an easy sharing of job experience and information as members discover more efficient and effective ways of doing their jobs.

The members of Work Group A and Group B both perform the same task. That task is neither integrated nor interactive to any significant degree. But the difference in their performances results because Work Group A is more like a team than Work Group B— and because Work Group A has *decided* to become a team.

Work Group A developed into a team not because of its environment or the requirements of task performance. Team development was not imposed. Team development was chosen.

Superior Work Teams

The relationships between work groups, work teams, and superior work teams are developmental. All organizational units that combine in some way the work of more than one person start out as work groups. Work groups may develop into work teams. Work teams may develop into superior work teams. Work teams belong to a higher level in the performance hierarchy than work groups and work teams.

The more a work group is characterized by the following, the more it has become a work team:

- It achieves certain distinctive **Results.**

- It employs successfully certain kinds of informal work **Processes.**

- It develops in their members certain kinds of **Feelings.**

- It develops **Leadership** that focuses both on team development and on team performance.

Superior work teams have the same functional and qualitative characteristics as work teams—and more. Superior work teams carry these characteristics to higher levels of development. Superior work teams achieve special levels of **consistency, intensity,** and **restless dissatisfaction.**

Consistency

When people describe the superior teams to which they belong, they use words like *always* and *never.*

- "We always kept everyone informed about changes in the flow sequence."

- "Training never took a back seat to anything else. We knew that if we didn't stay out in front on the learning curve, we would soon pay the price in new ideas and products."

Superior work teams are consistent in their pursuit of excellence. Quality isn't a fad, and they don't live by slogans. They live by their constancy. They are in their jobs and their business for the long haul. A member of a design team reported having had this experience:

I remember once when our team was really up against it, and we were beginning to break apart and talk about giving up. One of our technicians piped up and said, "Maybe if we spent more time working the problem rather than trying to convince ourselves to give up, we'd get somewhere."

Superior work teams

- *always* make maximum use of their people;
- *always* achieve superior outputs against all odds; and
- *always* are improving every aspect of their business.

Figure 1–2 displays the relationship between work groups, work teams, and superior work teams.

Intensity

The level of energy and commitment in superior work teams is measurably higher than it is in other work units. When you are in the midst of such a team, you find people who are extremely impatient. They are impatient with such things as

- unsolved problems
- excuses
- irrational delays
- distractions
- poor preparation
- lack of focus, and
- trivia of any kind.

Teams that have great intensity sometimes develop a whole set of catch-phrases and symbols. During the meetings of one team, if a member started to say something and began with a long preamble, another member would interject, "Don't wind up—just pitch." A project team posted its "top ten" problems that daily stood in the critical path of its pert chart. Each morning, "top ten" badges were handed out to the technicians and engineers who had the responsibility to fix problems. They wore these badges until they fixed the

Characteristics	Work Groups	Work Teams	Superior Work Teams
Functional	Teamwork exists only as task performance requires integrative or interactive processes.	Teamwork exists in most task performance processes and in most areas of team management.	Teamwork exists in **all** task performance processes and in all areas of team management.
Qualitative	Teamwork is rarely characterized by consistency, intensity, and restless dissatisfaction.	Teamwork is often characterized by consistency, intensity, and restless dissatisfaction.	Teamwork is **always** characterized by consistency, intensity, and restless dissatisfaction.

Figure 1–2. *Relationships of Work Groups, Work Teams, and Superior Work Teams*

problems. The badges were not punitive; rather, they signaled to everyone else in the project that the person wearing one was working a critical path problem and had a call on any other project member for whatever that person needed.

In one of my seminars, a member of a fabrication team described his experience on his superior team:

> When we committed to the idea that quality took precedence over everything—I mean like productivity and profit and everything else—we never turned back. I don't remember a single time of letting a job leave our shop that came back because of our work.

Restless Dissatisfaction

People who have talked to me about their superior work teams have
said things like

- "I remember all too well one poster on the wall: 'If it ain't
  broke, improve it.' "

- "Everything was always fair game. Nothing was sacred. We
  could question how anything was being done anytime."

Some time ago, while I was driving my six-year-old great-
nephew to school, I was struck by the similarity of his behavior
and that of members of superior work teams. Six-year-olds and
superior-work-team members have one thing in common. They ask,
"Why?" And what is more, they ask it all the time. Some work
teams have so legitimated and institutionalized "Why?" that they
use "Why Diagrams" in their team problem-solving sessions.

Superior work teams, like work teams,

- achieve certain distinctive Results;

- successfully employ certain kinds of Informal Processes;

- develop in their members certain kinds of Feelings; and

- enjoy a special kind of Leadership that acts through teamwork
  and focuses on both development and performance.

But superior work teams add to these characteristics the qualitatively different dimensions of consistency, intensity, and restless
dissatisfaction. They are functionally and qualitatively different
from work teams. They are functionally different in that they produce superior results, manage more of their team's work processes
and performance, and undertake more systematically the ongoing
tasks of team development.

In the following chapters, I will develop in detail a model for
superior-work-team development and performance. The model describes what all work teams are like to some degree, but it describes
what superior work teams are always like because of their consistency, intensity, and restless dissatisfaction.

Summary

This chapter has developed definitions for key terms that used throughout the rest of the book: **teamwork, work group, work team,** and **superior work team.**

Teamwork

Teamwork can exist

- in permanent work groups;

- in temporary groups (proposal teams, tiger teams, accident investigation teams, and the like);

- among units of the same organization and among units of different organizations; and

- in informal networks by which information and resources are exchanged.

Teamwork describes

- a highly desirable condition that may not be permanent and that can exist for any period of time—long or short—in any group;

- the *qualitative* characteristics of groups like being closely knit together around a common purpose, working easily together, and having positive work relationships.

- the *functional* characteristics of groups that must work together and cooperate in order to produce a product or service that cannot be produced by a single person.

- the multitude of Actions, Informal Processes, Feelings, and Results that distinguish work groups from work teams and work teams from superior work teams.

Work Groups

Work groups are units of two or more jobholders

- that typically do not exceed thirty people;
- whose leadership role is usually filled by one person;
- in which the work of individual group members is performed through processes that are additive, integrative, or interactive; and
- that are the primary unit of performance in the organization.

Work Teams

Work teams are functionally and qualitatively different from work groups. They are functionally different in that

- work teams do things that work groups don't do, and
- members of work teams not only cooperate in all aspects of their task performance, they all share in what are traditionally thought of as management functions. That is, they share responsibilities for joint planning, organizing the team, setting performance goals, assessing the team's performance, developing their own strategies to manage change, and securing their own resources.

They are qualitatively different from work groups in that

- when work teams do what work groups do, they add value; that is, the sharing of information is easier, issues are aired openly, and conflicts are resolved quickly and with positive results.

Four fundamental characteristics of work teams are:

- They achieve certain distinctive *Results*.
- They successfully employ certain kinds of *Informal Processes*.

- They develop in their members certain kinds of Feelings.
- They develop *Leadership* that focuses both on team development and team performance.

Superior Work Teams

Superior work teams have all the characteristics of work teams, but these characteristics are extremely persistent and are developed to an extraordinary degree. Superior work teams differ from work teams by virtue of their:

- consistency
- intensity, and
- restless dissatisfaction.

2
Team Building and Team Development—
What's the Difference?

T his book is intended to give managers and other key people in organizations a practical and powerful tool for developing superior work teams. Two key concepts must be fully understood in order to provide the kind of practical direction that managers and other key people need to develop superior work teams. These concepts are *superior work teams* and *development*. In chapter 1, I defined superior work teams and highlighted that definition by comparing superior work teams with work groups and work teams. In this chapter I will define what I mean by development and then describe my Model for Super Team Development and Performance and how to use it.

Confusion of Terms

There is general confusion in the way the terms **team building** and **team development** are used by researchers, consultants, managers, and the rank and file. The two terms are sometimes combined in the titles of training programs, such as "Team Building and Team Development Training," "Training Managers to Build and Develop Teams," and "Building and Developing Teams for The Future." Authors who write about team building and team development also tend to use the terms interchangeably (cf. Dyer 1977 and Varney 1989).

But some very useful distinctions should be made between team building and team development, distinctions that can give managers and other key people considerable guidance in carrying out their responsibilities as team leaders. From my own experience as a management educator and organizational consultant, I can certainly attest that recognizing these critical distinctions between team building and team development leads one to consider strategies for improving work teams that would otherwise be overlooked.

Some Fundamental Distinctions

The functional differences between team building (TBld) and team development (TDev) are extremely useful in guiding team-development actions. These four distinctions are displayed in figure 2–1 and can be defined as follows:

1. TBld focuses on the team's deficits. TDev focuses on the team's positive opportunities for continuous improvement.

2. TBld is short term. TDev is long term.

3. TBld is intense. TDev is diffused.

4. TBld primarily targets improving relationships on the team itself. TDev targets improvements in all organizational and team systems.

Deficit versus Positive Opportunity

Team building focuses on **deficits** in team performance and its primary goal is remedial—to fix something. Team development does not assume that something is wrong and should be fixed but proceeds on the expectation that there are always **positive opportunities** for improvement.

Team building begins with some perceived problem and proceeds through the steps of data gathering, diagnosis, remedial planning, implementation, and evaluation.

Some years ago I was asked to assist the national office of

Team building	Team development
Deficit focus on blocks to team's performance	Focuses on positive opportunities for continuous improvement in performance
Short-term concern; emphasis on fixing immediate problems	Long-term concern, emphasis on setting up systems for the long haul.
Intense; usually varies from a few hours to a few days	Diffused and ongoing, a part of the day-to-day processes of work
Typically targets problems in the relationships among team members	Targets creating and improving all the team's systems to insure they support sustained superior performance and continuous development

Figure 2–1. *Distinctions Between Team Building and Team Development*

a large Protestant denomination to create a self-managed team-building package to be used in multiple church staffs. In the preface to the team-building handbook that I prepared, I wrote that team building should be understood "as a process of intentional and planned activities which focus on: (1) resolving problems that result from team members working together; and (2) freeing team members to become maximally effective in accomplishing team goals."

I envisioned team building as a deficit-focused process. The process I proposed rested on the assumption that there were deficits in multiple church staff teams in the way they were structured, in the way power was used, in the way team members interacted, and in the way people communicated and resolved conflict.

Two years ago, I was asked to assist six proprietary organizations that had many organizational interfaces in sharing various responsibilities in a large engineering project. There were many indications that team building was needed; many problems in communication and cooperation had surfaced since the project began. The team-building interventions that I designed and conducted were clearly focused on performance deficits.

In collecting data from which to begin my interventions, I assumed that there were problems to be resolved. My surveys and my interviews, in one form or another, asked people for their perceptions of what was wrong.

The number of things that can go wrong in a work unit is probably infinite. Some of the more common problems, however, that become the occasion for team building are:

- Communication—people don't disclose what they know that could help each other; suggestions and ideas are not welcomed; hidden agendas abound; and there is a lot of secrecy about company plans, personnel actions, and the like.

- Decision making—people are regularly surprised by changes in their organizational relationships and responsibilities; most people affected by these decisions are not consulted beforehand.

- Lack of disagreement and risk taking—people play it safe; they have a lot of unexpressed hostility.

- Criticism of people's motives and intentions—people are assumed not to really care or to be inept, foolish, or indifferent.

- Open conflict—people fight to protect their turf; they refuse to cooperate with each other; they often spend a lot of energy just avoiding each other; they go out of their way to create obstacles for each other; they enjoy one another's failures.

- Destructive competition—individuals and work groups perceive themselves to be in a win-lose contest with others; individual goals are pursued at the expense of corporate ones.

- Scapegoating and abdication of personal responsibility—people excuse and rationalize their own mistakes; they don't have ownership of the team's goals or decisions; people spend a lot of energy in protecting their own power and security.

If TBld is focused on "fixing something that is broke," then TDev is focused on "making something better that ain't broke." It is no accident that TDev is the preferred way that organizations describe what they are doing about teams in their TQM initiatives. Many organizations, long before they undertake TQM initiatives, have prided themselves on always functioning as teams. They see TQM, therefore, as an opportunity to focus not on deficits of team performance but on positive opportunities to fulfill the potential that their teams have only partially realized.

Much time in TQM programs is used to create the capability for long-term improvement, such as in training teams to use new techniques and strategies for continuous improvement.

In TDev, teams that are already accustomed to solving problems are given better techniques like statistical process control, work simplification, and structured problem analysis. Managers who already think of themselves as team players and team leaders are taught how to listen more effectively and how to be better coaches (Kinlaw 1989).

Team building is an important set of interventions in the ongoing process of team development. Sometimes blocks to a team's performance emerge that must be responded to immediately. Team building encompasses a process and a set of strategies for doing just this. Team development, however, is a team's ongoing process of continuous improvement as it moves from one plateau to the next higher one. TBld focuses on deficits, whereas TDev focuses on positive opportunities for even more effective performance. The relationship between team building and team development is displayed in figure 2–2.

Short Term versus Long Term

TBld is a specific intervention that appears called for because a problem in team performance has surfaced, such as conflict, lack of goal clarity, or inequitable power distribution. TBld is **short term.** It invariably takes place with the team assembled. TDev describes the **long-term process** of continuous improvement and therefore cannot occur in one meeting or a series of meetings.

Clearly, the notions of Deficit versus Positive Opportunity and

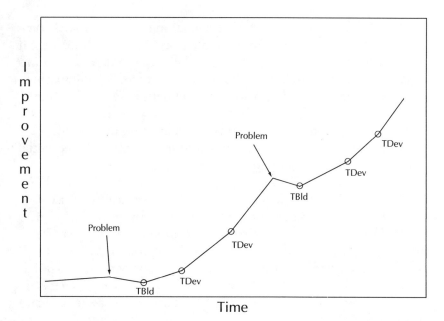

Figure 2–2. *Relationship of Team-Building to Team-Development Actions*

Short Term versus Long Term are related. If TBld is a form of treatment for ailing teams, TDev is a team's design for continued good health and improvement.

TBld identifies a set of short-term changes and improvements that we expect to take hold and become imbedded in the warp and weft of organizational life. TDev includes all the routine daily, routinized actions that a team uses to continue its unending upward progress toward improved performance.

A few years back I was asked to consult with a financial group. Some of the presenting problems were a 100 percent turnover in staff during the previous eighteen months; virulent backbiting and criticism of the firm's two partners by employees; open, injurious conflict between the two partners; scapegoating; and fault-finding. The firm was on the verge of breaking apart.

After a preliminary analysis and diagnosis of the problems, the first step was to "stop the bleeding." I engaged in several TBld interventions just to get people in a frame of mind to work together and to begin the process of improvement. My first session was a weekend retreat for the two partners. The following Monday the partners had an all-hands meeting and publicly confronted some of the destructive ways that the two of them had been behaving. I continued the TBld sessions with the partners and embarked on regular TBld sessions with all employees.

Once the firm had been stabilized, people began to believe that improvement was possible, I began to put in place TDev processes for the long haul.

With full participation of partners and the employees, we developed a strategic plan that explicitly identified teamworking as a dominant value of the firm. Until I began working with the firm, there had been no systematic, explicit process of performance evaluation and reward. One of the next things that happened was that the employees, on their own, developed an appraisal and reward system. The system was presented to the firm's partners, and they approved it.

When I first started my TBld intervention with this firm, we would make one step forward and two steps back. At a team-building session on Monday we would make a little progress on trust and reducing some of the acts of interpersonal sabotage, only to find that by the end of the week, we were back to ground zero again. But as we continued the TBld sessions, we were able to stabilize our gains. Once the effects of TBld were realized, I was able to initiate the TDev actions for the long haul.

Both TBld and TDev are integral to creating and maintaining work teams and for transforming work teams into superior work teams. For quite functional reasons, TBld should be thought of as a set of deficit-focused, short-term actions. TDev, on the other hand, should be thought of as including all actions that institutionalize the processes by which teams continue to become better and better.

Intense versus Diffused

Because TBld is focused on a deficit and is short term, TBld interventions are **intense.**

TBld interventions invariably take place in extended meetings, sometimes lasting for days. The attitude that most often marks the climate of TBld is, "Nobody leaves until we fix the problem." Indeed, one of the major dangers in TBld sessions is that more problems will emerge than can be managed in the time allowed.

A consultant was running a TBld session some years ago for a Roman Catholic bishop and his diocesan staff. During the first few hours of the TBld retreat, the consultant was facilitating the group and helping it to identify the problems that it wished to discuss and fix during the TBld session. The group identified some fifty problems. After the consultant had listed the fifty problems, he used a bit of humor to help the group realize that it had to narrow the list way down in order to have some hope of fixing at least something during the session. The consultant told the group the following story.

> I am reminded of the old priest who was on a cathedral staff in a university town. Not only did he have responsibilities at the cathedral, but he also taught several classes at the university and had, therefore, given students many, many tests. His text on Sunday for his sermon happened to be the Ten Commandments. After he had read all ten of the commandments he unconsciously looked up from his text and peered out over his glasses to the congregation and said (from force of habit in giving exams to his students): "Of course, not all ten should be attempted in the time allotted."

TBld sessions can become quite confrontational in nature. Often they are designed to be just that. The goal may be to stimulate as much interaction and to obtain as many different points of view as possible. At the very minimum, such sessions can have no immediate effect unless people honestly voice their opinions and demonstrate their true feelings.

It is not uncommon for TBld sessions to run for long, uninterrupted hours and well into the night. Because they are characterized by a sense of urgency, they are usually intense.

One obvious reason that TBld sessions are intense is that they take place within a very circumscribed time frame. TBld sessions have a beginning and an end. Participants know from the start of a TBld session that they have a certain amount of time to finish their work. They know that they must make use of the time allotted or risk missing an important opportunity—one that they may not have again.

TDev, in contrast to TBld, focuses on continuous improvement, and it coexists as a way of life with everything a team does. TDev therefore lacks the intensity of TBld. It is **diffused** among all the processes, actions, values, and practices of a team.

The goal of TDev is to make itself completely unobtrusive. Teams should look to the time that they no longer use the term *team development* to identify a set of special or specific actions. TDev, like quality, must finally become a way of life in all work groups.

For example, all teams should engage in strategic planning. All teams should capitalize on consensual decision making. All teams should force as many decisions as far down in their organizations as possible. All teams should focus themselves on total customer satisfaction and continuous improvement in all their work pro-cesses. Team development includes all these long-term operations, whose impact is diffused throughout every aspect of the team's life.

As teams step out onto the long and endless road of team devel-opment, it is useful for them to talk about TDev actions and oppor-tunities. At some point, however, I would expect teams to simply think of these actions as the way they routinely do business.

We can make the best use of TBld and TDev if we understand that they describe two separate strategies for helping teams perform up to their full potential. TBld focuses on the deficits and shortfalls in a team's performance. TDev focuses on positive opportunities for improving what is already working. TBld is short term and in-tense. TDev is long term and diffused. Finally, TBld primarily tar-gets improvements in relationships, whereas TDev targets improve-ments in systems.

Relational versus Systemic

I can remember undertaking no TBld action that did not have to resolve problems in human relationships. My experience is obvi-ously echoed in that of many others. The first three items in a Team Development Scale commonly used by consultants (Dyer 1977) have to do with relationships: "To what extent do I feel part of the team?" "How safe is it in this team to be at ease, relaxed, and myself?" "To what extent do I feel 'under wraps,' that is, have private thoughts, unspoken reservations, or unexpressed opinions that I have not felt comfortable bringing into the open?" Two more of the ten items on the questionnaire also address interpersonal relationships on the team: "How are differences or conflicts handled in our team?" "How do people relate to the team leader, chairman or 'boss'?"

By far, most published information about team building and team development focuses on some aspect of team-member **relationships.** We are fortunate, therefore, that a lot of information is available on communication, cohesiveness, conflict resolution, and the like. These are important resources for designing and implementing TBld actions.

TDev, as distinguished from TBld, is directed at **systems** and is concerned with questions like: What kind of reward system fosters long-term team development? What kind of appraisal system supports team development? What are the roles and functions of supervisors in encouraging team development?

When McDonnell Douglas recently embarked on its TQM initiative, it recognized that a complete overhaul of management and supervision was required. Before it could expect to get TQM off the ground, it had to redefine the role of supervisor as a team player and begin a process of radical change in the organization's culture.

Team development represents such a process of transformation. It includes strategies that get at a company's values, its human resource development plan, its appraisal and reward systems, its organizational structure, its practices, and its policies. One company that has apparently begun to realize the potential of team development is General Motors' Cadillac engine plant at Livonia, Michigan (Nora et al. 1986).

The result of the long-term, diffused team-development processes used at Livonia has been a transformation.

Imagine an American plant with no executive parking or dining areas, no general foreman, relatively few support staff, no multi-classification systems for job descriptions and compensation, workers (all union members) divided into teams with responsibility for production, quality control, materials handling, and the like. Further imagine the whole had been planned by a committee on which sat four union members as active participants. A figment of the imagination? Not at all. It is . . . a new American paradigm for production.

Summary

There is considerable confusion about the meaning of *team building* and *team development*. At least two conditions have contributed to this confusion:

- no distinction is made between team development and team building, and the two terms are used interchangeably; and

- team-development models do not start with team performance.

A set of logical distinctions should be made between team building and team development. Functional distinctions between team building and team development have proven extremely useful in my own experience of guiding TBld and TDev initiatives. These four distinctions are displayed in figure 2–1 and figure 2–2.

1. TBld focuses on team deficits. TDev focuses on positive opportunities for continuous improvement.

2. TBld is short term. TDev is long term.

3. TBld is intense. TDev is diffused.

4. TBld primarily targets improving relationships on the team. TDev targets improvements in all organizational and team systems.

This book is not about team building, but team development. No designs and techniques for conducting team-building meetings appear in the pages that follow. Rather, there is information about the iterative, long-term task of developing teams that consistently produce superior results.

When team development bogs down, a group has run into some kind of obstacle. It may have to undertake a short-term, intense set of actions to remove the obstacle, such as TBld. But for continuous improvement and sustained superior performance to be established as a way of life, there are no quick fixes. Nothing short of a transformation through team development will do. The rest of this book shows team leaders how to make that transformation.

3
Overview of the Model for Superior Team Development and Performance

The Model for Superior Team Development and Performance is a functional model. It describes superior work teams and suggests what leaders and other key players can do to build them. Ideas and strategies to translate the model into action are found in later chapters, but this chapter introduces the model and sketches its elements and their relationships to each other.

A number of team-development and team-performance models have been described by other writers (cf. Hackman 1983; Kolodny and Kiggundu 1980; Nieva et al. 1985; Steiner 1972; Thamhain and Wilemon 1987). I have referred to these models in conducting my own studies of work teams and have taken them into account in constructing my own Model for Superior Team Development and Performance. My model, however, differs in several special ways from others. Its important and distinctive characteristics are:

- The model does not view team development and performance as finally dependent on the nature of the task or the quality of the environment. It sees that team development and performance as largely a function of a work unit's decision to be a team—regardless of task and environment.

- The model couples development with performance. The issues for team development and team performance are the same. Team development and team performance occur together—the better the team the better the performance.

- The model is built upon a clear distinction between team build-ing and team development.

- The model emphasizes aspects that other models do not, such as Informal Processes and Feelings.

- The model does not just describe teams—it describes superior teams.

Characteristics of the Model

I have set out to construct a model that:

- is easily understood;

- is "lean" and includes only information that will produce the most dramatic results;

- shows team development and performance as fully integrated activities;

- provides an outline for designing superior-work-team develop-ment and ensuring superior performance; and

- easily generates team-specific actions for securing the quality and competitive edge.

Easily Understood

The model describes four elements that most people mention when they talk about their best teams: Results, Informal Processes, Feel-ings, and Leadership. (The fifth element in the model, Key Strate-gies, is not part of the model proper.) The four elements of Results, Informal Processes, Feelings, and Leadership reflect the experiences of the majority of people who have actually been members of work teams. The model describes exactly what people must take into ac-count if they want to have superior work teams. There is no one definite sequence that work groups and work teams must follow in developing themselves into superior work teams. But they must

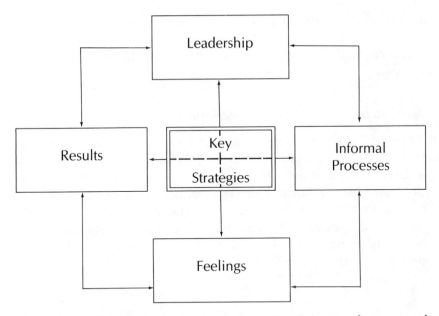

Figure 3–1. *Elements in the Model for Superior Team Development and Performance*

address all four elements in the model, focusing on Results, Informal Processes, Feelings, and Leadership (figure 3–1).

Unless indicated otherwise, when I refer to the model I will be referring to the four primary elements. The Key Strategies element is included to describe specific ways to strengthen the four primary elements.

Lean

The model includes the bare-bones minimum of what must be taken into account in order to stimulate superior-work-team development and ensure superior performance. Only four primary elements in the model describe the characteristics of superior teams, but there are doubtlessly others that have an impact on team development and performance. Often these other elements are outside the influence of team members. Everything in the model highlights opportunities that every work unit can address. It does not include variables that work teams may not be able to influence, such as the total organizational environment or the nature of the tasks to be performed.

Integrating Development and Performance

The model explicitly declares that team development and team performance are inseparable. To develop is to perform. To undertake a developmental activity is to take an action that becomes part of the team's performance. For example, if a team decides to better use its members' competencies, it is making a decision not only about its development but one that will ensure improvement in the quality of its products and services. If a team begins to calibrate its own performance, it will invariably identify opportunities for its development.

A Model by Which to Design

The model clearly targets potential opportunities for developing teams and improving performance. Within each of the primary elements, a number of subelements or opportunities are listed that help define exactly what work units should focus on to become superior teams. For example, four Informal Processes are listed: communicating and contacting; responding and adapting; influencing and improving; and appreciating and celebrating. Each of these processes becomes a checkpoint in building a superior-team-development initiative. All the subelements listed under each of the other three elements can be used in a similar way. These subelements are the critical leverage points for superior team development.

Identifying Specific Strategies

The model summarizes the actual experiences that people have had when they were engaged in some type of superior teamwork or were members of superior work teams. It has been stripped down to only the most essential information. Because of these two qualities, the model can easily be translated into very concrete strategies relevant to the needs of any team.

For example, an engineering design group that was in a seminar of mine decided that it should strengthen the way it showed appreciation to its team members and celebrated individual and team successes. The team described its current condition, and the members had all kinds of illustrations of their expectations. They decided exactly what kind of actions they needed to take, and the result was they more than doubled the number of formal awards that they obtained for their team and infused a lot more creative energy into their informal award system.

The model I am proposing focuses only on work units that do real work in real organizations. It can be applied to at least the following kinds of teams:

- management teams
- permanent work teams
- temporary and special-purpose teams, and
- interface teams.

The model applies to critical-care units in hospitals, quality assurance groups, accounting units, government offices, and multiple staffs of religious organizations, as well as to chief executive officers and their staff. It applies to any work unit that produces outputs for an internal or external customer and that stays together long enough to assume responsibility for its own team development. Groups that meet only once or twice are too short lived to undertake any significant team development initiatives.

Primary Elements of the Model

Figure 3–1 outlines the primary elements in the Model for Superior Team Development and Performance and suggests their interactive and interdependent relationships. The four primary elements are:

1. **Achieving Superior Team Results.** Results are the final outcomes of making maximum use of a team's human re-

sources; delivering outputs of superior services and products (even against all odds); showing continuous improvement; and building enthusiastically positive customers.

2. **Helping Informal Team Processes to Emerge.** Informal Processes are the day-to-day processes of communicating and contacting, responding and adapting, influencing and improving, and appreciating and celebrating.

3. **Nurturing Positive Team Feelings.** Among the most important of such Feelings are inclusion, commitment, loyalty, pride, and trust.

4. **Developing Leadership that Is Focused on Both Team Development and Team Performance.** Among the special roles that superior-work-team leaders fulfill are Initiator, Model, and Coach.

Team Results

When people talk about the achievements of their superior teams they use phrases like

- "We sacrificed personal needs and interests to reach a common goal."

- "We were always trying to do things better. Sometimes you felt like every few weeks you were using so many new techniques that you were in a different job."

- "What I remember most was the way the people who used our trouble-shooting service felt about us. They thought we walked on water."

- "When people finally knocked off, we looked like a moving company or a bunch of computer salesmen or something. People took their PCs home at night and did all sorts of new things."

- "We all worked very hard, there wasn't much slack, we were on a tight schedule."

- "We never gave up, we always found a way to work around obstacles, to solve problems, to fix things."
- "We simply did a superior job and outperformed everybody's expectations."
- "We could be flexible. We weren't bound by so many rules that we couldn't be inventive."
- "There was a lot of excitement. Things were always happening. You could almost feel the energy at times."

Such comments as these (and hundreds of others) indicate that superior work teams consistently accomplish at least the following four Results (figure 3–2):

- maximum use of the team's human resources;
- superior outputs against all odds; and
- continuous improvement.

Maximum Use of the Team's Human Resources

People describe their superior work team's performance as an effort in which their competencies (motivation, knowledge, skill, and experience) and those of their colleagues were fully utilized—everyone gave a hundred and ten percent. The whole group was energized. People felt driven to succeed.

The people in my studies have talked about "being stretched." They talk about "doing the impossible," of "pulling off an incredible coup," of "breakthroughs," and of "feeling bigger than life." They describe learning new skills and developing new insights. People on superior teams are stimulated to think, to solve problems, and to know more about their total organizations than they ever dreamed possible. Members of superior work teams have the experience of transcending themselves—of going beyond what they thought were permanent limitations.

Superior Outputs against All Odds

When people talk about their best teams, they describe their Results as exceeding expectations—of going beyond what they and others

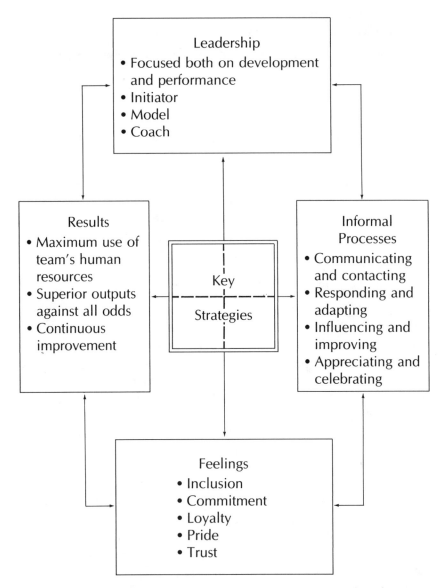

Figure 3–2. *The Model for Superior Team Development and Performance*

thought was possible. They talk about being flexible and innovative and of never giving up.

In superior work teams the adrenaline is flowing, energy levels are high, and members approach their jobs with the expectation that together they will find a way to meet the most difficult and unexpected challenges.

Continuous Improvement

People often remember their times on superior work teams as ones in which they were always reaching a bit higher and challenging the limits. They remember reducing error rates, changing work-flow processes, improving customer satisfaction, and increasing output.

Continuous improvement is currently being introduced to thousands of American jobholders throughout the private and public sector as a key element in TQM. But none of the various TQM processes and techniques will catch on and be applied except in work teams. All such techniques and processes require high levels of communication and contact, response and adaptation, and coordination and sequencing. They require, in short, the environment that can be supplied only by superior work teams.

One characteristic Result where continuous improvement occurs for superior work teams is customer satisfaction. Superior work teams consistently create enthusiastically positive customers who depend on their services and products.

All work units have customers—other people within and without the organization who use their services and products. One mark of poorly performing work units is that they fail to recognize that they have customers. And they certainly don't make the important distinction between satisfied customers and enthusiastically positive customers. Superior work teams do know that they have customers, and they are obsessive about giving their customers each time—and every time—services and products fully fit to use.

Superior work teams create superior customers. They do it, first, by providing products and services that are fully fit to use; second, by maintaining a continuous feedback and follow-up process with their customers; and third, by maintaining a process of continuous quality improvement.

The first practical question that leaders and members of groups should answer is, What difference does it make if we work at being a team? The answer is that they will simply produce better outputs. Superior work teams make superior companies—that is, companies that will gain and keep the quality and competitive edge.

The next question to answer is, What do teams do to achieve such outputs? One very important thing they do is that they create and use a set of very distinctive Informal Processes.

Figure 3–2 provides an overview of the complete Model for Superior Team Development and Performance, showing each major element and its component parts.

Informal Team Processes

At least four routine Informal Processes that superior work teams use are thoroughly ingrained in the way they do business. These processes are not formal systems, like performance appraisal, work sequencing, and reporting requirements. But all formal systems are influenced and made more functional and effective by certain processes that help form the environment within which the team operates. The four Informal Processes that help transform work groups and work teams into superior work teams are:

- communicating and contacting
- responding and adapting
- influencing and improving, and
- appreciating and celebrating.

Communicating and Contacting

Members of superior work teams talk a lot, interact a lot, and meet a lot. They talk to each other and to other team members. Most of all, they talk to their customers—inside and outside their organizations.

Superior-work-team members spend time with each other on and off the job. I saw a sign in a company recently that read: "Work hard, play hard—and do them together." One key to the enormous success that the Springfield Re-manufacturing Company has reported has to do with nothing more complicated than (as its vice president put it) "managers and employees playing together."

Responding and Adapting

Members of superior work teams respond to each other, to problems, to challenges, and to the unexpected—and often in highly creative ways.

They are quick to recognize changes as possible opportunities, not to resist them as catastrophes. Some superior work teams seem actually to thrive on adversity. They make new discoveries, find new allies, and develop clever ways to work around problems.

One team of senior managers that I was assisting in a strategic planning initiative was informed during one of our sessions that corporate headquarters was planning to levy a ten-percent cut in overhead expenses across the board for all its regional offices. Rather than going into an "ain't it awful" episode (the typical response), this team decided to plan a twenty-percent cut, then work back up to a ten-percent cut. The logic was that if they could manage really bad news like a twenty-percent cut, a ten-percent cut would be a cup of tea.

Influencing and Improving

Superior work teams make it easy for people to influence every aspect of the team's work. It follows from this that these teams are always on a positive improvement slope. When people join superior work teams, they sometimes must make quite an adjustment. One jobholder described it this way to me:

> I had been on board for less than a week when we had our first staff meeting. My group was in the process of analyzing a particular work flow sequence for handling materials in a metals processing sequence. I knew just enough to be feel ignorant. But everyone expected me to join in. In fact the other people made it impossible to keep silent. They kept asking me, "what do you think?" I had more say in that group in the first half hour than I had in the years I had been in my previous job.

In most work units, whether they are teams or not, members have some degree of influence over their jobs. In superior work teams, member influence includes every aspect of the team's life and work.

In the traditional work unit, the jobholder is responsible for his or her job, and the supervisor is responsible for the unit. In superior work teams all the members can influence all aspects of the team's performance, so all members feel responsible for all aspects of the team's performance. In traditional work groups, the "experts" solve problems. In superior work teams, everyone solves problems.

Influence is inevitably coupled with continuous improvement. As one manager put it, "There is nothing more complicated in improving a job than asking the people who do the job how to improve it."

My experience has verified that manager's statement many times over. I ask jobholders attending my seminars to jot down one idea that they firmly believe could improve the quality of their organization's performance. I don't know of a single case in which every person has not written down an idea.

Then I ask the same jobholders to answer the following question: "Do you believe that, if you made your improvement suggestion to your boss, you would get a thoughtful hearing?" Less than twenty-five percent of them answer yes.

Superior work teams consistently make the most of their human resources. One reason for this is that they make it easy for people to be influential and to improve everything the team does.

Appreciating and Celebrating

Another Informal Process that superior teams use is appreciating and celebrating. Members of superior work teams typically work long and even stressful hours. They talk about being tired and sometimes exhausted. But they also talk about their experiences as ones in which they were respected and highly thought of. They remember receiving a lot of kudos and pats on the back.

Members of superior work teams don't take each other for granted. When people take on the tough and dirty jobs, their peers and their leaders say thank you. And they do it in some pretty creative, if not outrageous ways.

One of my favorite awards is used by Grumman's technical services division. It's called the Quiet Excellence Award. Any team member can nominate another member for the award. It is given to people who consistently perform their jobs in an outstanding manner without complaint or fanfare.

The first functional characteristic of superior work teams that distinguishes them from other work units is that they consistently produce superior results. The second is that they employ at least four distinctive Informal Processes of:

- communicating and contacting
- responding and adapting
- influencing and improving, and
- appreciating and celebrating.

Informal Processes and Results are clearly related and interactive. By communicating and staying in contact with each other, teams are using a process to make maximum use of their human resources. By staying in close communication with their customers, they are using an important strategy to insure enthusiastically positive customers. By responding and adapting, superior work teams are using a fundamental process for making continuous improvement part of the routine way they do business.

There are two other sets of characteristics of superior teams that are interrelated with Results and Informal Processes. Superior-work-team members share a set of common Feelings about their work and their team, and they develop Leadership that is implemented through teamwork and that stays focused on both team development and team performance.

Team Feelings

People who describe their experiences on superior work teams usually give implicit and explicit information about how they felt as members of their teams. The kinds of remarks they make are:

- "Nobody was left out—we all felt that we were in this thing together."

- "We respected each other, we took each other's ideas seriously, nobody got put down."

- "You felt as if you could count on the other people. If they said they were going to do something, they did it."

- "Sometimes it felt like a family. We were really close."

- "People didn't hide anything. We kept everything above board. If something wasn't right and people were not getting along, we fixed it."

- "People didn't try to embarrass each other. It was as if people went out of their way to make somebody else look good."

- "We were like a juggernaut. There was no way anybody was going to get in our way."

- "Sometimes you had to stop and remind yourself that you had a family and other things to take care of besides the job. It felt so important to get the job done that you sometimes forgot about everything else."

- "It was easy to get confused about who had what job. We all jumped in to take care of whatever needed doing."

- "You never had to ask for help. If someone had a little slack, they would start working with the person who was snowed under."

These and the hundreds of other statements reveal five Feelings that people describe so often that I have concluded they must be generally present among members of all superior work teams. These Feelings are inclusion, commitment, loyalty, pride, and trust.

Inclusion

Managers and employees who describe their experiences in superior work teams consistently use phrases like "There was a sense of togetherness," "No one felt left out," "Everyone shared in the tough times and the good times," "There was a real joy of being in the thing together," and "We had a real sense of camaraderie." Members feel *included* in the planning and problem-solving processes that affect them. They have access to the information they need, and they feel included in the work and purposes of the whole group.

Commitment

Team members also report feeling a strong sense of *commitment* to the team's goal and its success. They often describe this commitment by recording that team members sacrificed their personal needs.

As the manager of a subsystem in NASA's Viking Project put it, "For the duration of the project, I told my family that we were in this together. There was no way that our lives would go on as usual. Until launch, the project would be our first commitment."

Loyalty

A third Feeling that characterizes the experience of people on superior work teams is *loyalty* to the team and to each other. In a rocket-flow processing group, a technician told this story:

> Charlie was very sick. We didn't know when he would get back. We had a tough choice to make. Our group leader offered to get us a replacement. But we just couldn't do that to Charlie. We said we would catch up the slack until Charlie was back on his feet. And we did, but it cost each of us some Saturdays and Sundays to do it.

A senior executive described his best team experience this way:

> What I really remember about my directorate was that you never took cheap shots at anybody. And if you even tried to complain to a third party about another person or work group, you knew very quickly that the third party wasn't interested.

Pride

Members of superior work teams have a Feeling of pride. When I ask managers and employees what they mean by pride, they associate it with being successful against all kinds of obstacles and with doing something that was really meaningful. People do not believe that you can have good teams for long that consistently lose. Time and time again, during my interviews and seminars, managers and employees contrast their good teams with their bad ones. They remember bad experiences as those in which their teams failed to meet milestones, had large budget overruns, and took on projects that were later abandoned.

Trust

A fifth Feeling that people on superior work teams experience is trust. "When one of us said we would do something, you never had to ask again or follow up. You just knew it would be done" was the way a systems analyst put it.

A member of a logistics support group said of his team members, "We were all professionals. Every one of us was as good as you could get. If we didn't have the answers, there weren't any to be had."

Superior work teams have a distinctive team affect. Members feel different from members of other work units. They have very strong feelings of:

- inclusion
- commitment
- loyalty
- pride, and
- trust.

It isn't possible from my studies to tell which comes first—Feelings, Informal Processes, or Results—that is, whether a superior work team makes full use of its human resources and achieves superior performance, which then results in certain Feelings in team members, or vice versa. What is clear, however, is that superior work teams produce superior Results and employ distinctive Informal Processes and their members share a set of special Feelings. It is also clear that all these elements are in continuous interaction with each other.

In addition to Results, Informal Processes, and Feelings, superior work teams have a fourth distinguishing characteristic. They develop a special kind of Leadership.

A Special Kind Of Leadership

Leadership in superior teams is qualitatively different from leadership in other work units. In their performance and behavior, leaders in superior work teams emphasize a special set of roles and functions. These roles and functions can be performed by one person or by several persons.

In superior work teams Leadership is not primarily a use of power and influence to develop followers who respond in some desired way. It has, first of all, a radically different orientation from that of traditional leadership. It is accomplished as a team function, with and through the team. It is accomplished by women and men who are first, last, and always team players and team members. One member of an industrial shop describes his team leader this way:

> This guy was a team player all the way. He never played God or acted like he always knew best about everything. If we had a special project coming down, he always called us together to map out how we would take on the job. If anybody had an idea about how to make something better, he was always prepared to listen. And when we were doing some particularly dirty job, he was usually there pitching in and doing his bit.

Leadership in superior teams has two special meanings. It means

- leading through teamwork, and
- staying focused on both the team's development and team's performance.

Leading through Teamwork

Team leaders are team members and team players. They lead through teamwork. They view all work as an opportunity for teamwork. They view change as an opportunity for teamwork. The practical meaning of this orientation is that team leaders always focus:

- on team performance more than individual performance; and

- on commitment as the way to achieve superior performance, not control.

Staying Focused on Both the Team's Development and its Performance

Superior-work-team leaders see themselves as team members and use teamwork as their primary strategy for getting everything done. They also view team development and team performance as inseparable. They know that the more fully developed the team becomes, the better it will perform.

Superior leaders know that total performance is a function of the team's potential and that that potential is increased primarily through team development. Superior leaders give special attention to

- ensuring that the team is properly structured; and
- helping the team assess its own development as a team.

Structuring the Team. Structuring is the way to create clarity in a team about goals, objectives, priorities, job responsibilities, and procedures. Structuring also creates clarity about values and norms—that is, what people are expected to believe and how they are expected to behave.

Managers and employees describing their superior work teams *are much more likely to describe clarity about goals and values than they are to describe clarity about specific job responsibilities.* One programmer describes her experience this way:

> I don't think any of us were very clear at times who was supposed to do what. But then, nobody seemed to care. We just seemed to

work on whatever needed working on. It was a lot easier to tell my friends where I worked than it was to tell them what I did.

An engineer tells me:

The one sure way that you could shoot yourself in the foot was to keep a problem to yourself. If you had even the slightest idea that something downstream in the project was going to cause trouble, you were expected to make sure everybody concerned knew about it.

Superior-work-team leaders make a special effort to help their teams stay clear about norms and values.

Assessing the Team. Superior-work-team leaders also demonstrate their clear orientation toward both team development and team performance by helping the team track its own progress in developing as a team.

Comments from people about their best teams go like this:

- "Our leader always made sure we took time to ask ourselves how we were doing as a team and how we could improve our team."

- "We didn't just assume that we would naturally develop as a team. Our boss never let us forget that we had to do something about it, and that meant that we had to have some kind of a baseline against which to compare our progress."

- "We really worked at the business of being a team. We had a routine that we went through every Friday afternoon. Our shop foreman used a thing we called the three C's—communication, contact, and commitment. Everybody was expected to comment on anything that they thought was positive or negative in each area. It really made a difference just to keep those three ideas in front of everybody."

Superior-work-team leaders show their orientation toward both team development and team performance by ensuring that their teams are properly structured and by ensuring that their teams periodically assess their teams' development.

Leadership in superior teams has two fundamental meanings. It means

- leading through teamwork, and

- staying focused on both team development and team performance.

In addition to these two quite special orientations, superior-work-team leaders perform at least three special roles.

Superior Leadership Roles

At least three roles can be clearly associated with the leaders of superior work teams. These roles are:

- Initiator
- Model, and
- Coach.

Initiator. Superior leaders initiate the various actions and processes for building their work units into superior teams. The basic guideline for initiating team development is to make teamwork the norm for all their actions. They way they initiate team development is to involve the team at the very outset in the process.

Model. Superior-work-team leaders model the kind of performance and behavior that help develop their teams. In the simplest terms this means that they model what is expected of team members.

Team leaders model team membership in two ways. First, they model it in the way they conduct their own business and perform their own tasks. Second, they model it in the way they interact with their colleagues.

Coach. Coaching includes a multitude of informal conversations that team leaders have with individual team members or with groups of team members. In these conversations leaders carry out four distinguishable functions:

- They counsel and assist team members to clarify issues, develop alternative strategies, and resolve technical and personal problems.

- They mentor and help team members understand company politics, the values and biases of senior managers, and their own career opportunities.

- They tutor and help team members develop new technical and team skills.

- They (when necessary) confront and challenge team members to improve their performance and take on more challenging jobs.

The fifth and final element in the Model for Superior Team Development and Performance is Key Strategies for Superior Team Development and Performance.

Key Strategies

The Key Strategies by which a team can undertake the practical business of becoming superior include using

- **The Model for Superior Team Development and Performance,** as a tool for planning for team development and performance;

- **The Systems Model for Continuous Team Improvement,** to insure that improvement is comprehensive and integrated;

- **The Competencies and Influence Grid,** to ensure that a team is ensuring that team members are being fully utilized and are continuing to develop a new competencies; and

- **The Team Meeting Effectiveness Model** to help team members make the most of their planning and problem-solving meetings and to describe the kinds of skills that are required to make team meetings effective.

- **The Team Development Questionnaire,** which can be used to develop special initiatives to strengthen the five Feelings associated with superior-work-team development.

At this point I will not describe these particular strategies any further. I will, however, list some of the criteria I have used for selecting these Key Strategies.

First, each Strategy has been proven to have merit in various seminars and team development projects.

Second, the Strategies can be used only by teams. They force teamwork. They have little or no value if used by individuals in a unilateral action to improve their teams. *Teams can only improve through teamwork.*

Third, I have selected only Strategies that have a clear conceptual basis for action. Each Strategy is in fact a descriptive model that has various elements that are clearly related.

Fourth, these Key Strategies include only those that have multiple impacts on team development and performance; that is, each Strategy tends to improve team Results, Informal Processes, Feelings, and Leadership.

The Key Strategies are all ways to plan, organize and implement superior-work-team development.

The Model for Superior Team Development and Performance

There are four primary elements of superior work teams.

First, superior work teams produce Results that are quantitatively and qualitatively different from those of other work units. These Results include

- maximum use of team's human resources
- superior outputs against all odds, and
- continuous improvement.

Second, superior work teams use distinctive day-to-day Informal Processes like:

- communicating and contacting
- responding and adapting
- influencing and improving, and
- appreciating and celebrating.

Third, superior-work-team members have persistent positive Feelings of:

- inclusion
- commitment
- loyalty
- pride, and
- trust.

Fourth, superior teams develop Leadership that has special orientations:

- leading through teamwork, and

- staying focused on both team development and team performance.

Superior leaders also perform three special roles:

- Initiator
- Model, and
- Coach.

A fifth element is a set of proven Key Strategies for developing teams.

In figure 3–1 the primary elements of superior work teams are displayed to show their general relationship. The precise relationship among the four primary elements has not been established. But from the practical point of view, these relationships are not very important. What is important is:

- All the primary elements are interdependent, and to strengthen one is to strengthen all of the others.

- All the primary elements present targets of opportunity for developing superior teams.

- When the primary elements are taken in aggregate, they provide the basis for understanding and designing systematic and ongoing superior-work-team development.

Figure 3–2 gives a complete display of the Model for Superior Team Development and Performance. This model can best be understood in two ways:

1. It describes in part what consistently exists in superior teamwork.

2. It describes what consistently exists in superior work teams.

The model is based on information drawn from all kinds of work teams—administrative, research, production, financial, engineering, and service. It uses information from both the public and private sector. It uses information from teams that only sometimes have risen to the level of superior. It uses information from teams that have consistently demonstrated their superiority to other work units.

The model for Superior Team Development and Performance presents every manager and key player in every organization with a challenge. It demonstrates that the quality and competitive edge can be won by developing superior work teams, and it challenges managers to initiate and nurture that development.

In the following chapters I will describe each of the four primary elements in detail and show what specific things can be done to create these elements in any work group. I will follow the discussion of the four primary elements with a description of several strategies that can be used to develop superior teams.

4
Focusing on Results

For organizations, the major payoff of superior work teams is that they consistently produce superior Results. Organizations undertake strategies to develop superior work teams for the same reason they acquire new technologies, modify work sequences, and introduce management information systems. The reason is (or at least it should be) to achieve Results that ensure their long-term competitive position.

Results are the first primary element in the Model for Superior Team Development and Performance. The Results that superior work teams consistently achieve are:

- They make the **maximum use of their human resources.**

- They produce **superior outputs** (services and products) **against all odds.**

- They **continually improve** their total performance.

As we have seen, team development and team performance are not separate entities. The kind of performance that is required to-day—sustained superior performance—can come only from highly developed teams. Teamwork is the integrating activity in work units and organizations that leverages small improvements into very large ones. We can expect to achieve a competitive advantage only if we make full use of the integrating and transforming power that is po-tential in all work units.

Results, like the primary model elements, have both develop-mental and performance functions. When teams challenge them-selves by setting their sights on superior Results, they have initiated actions that both further their team development and improve their team performance.

When teams determine that they will create enthusiastically positive customers, they have explicitly targeted a superior Result, but they have also implicitly launched a process to develop themselves into the kind of team that can achieve such a Result.

Focusing on Results is a critical activity for superior-work-team development. I will show this by

- describing in some greater detail the Results that superior work teams achieve; and

- discussing some strategic considerations that should be taken into account when we focus on Results to improve team development and performance.

The first of the three Results that I will discuss is making maximum use of a team's human resources.

Maximum Use of a Team's Human Resources

Making the most of a team's human resources means giving people on the team the opportunity to use the competencies they have, and giving them chances to gain new competencies.

Competencies are the knowledge, skill, and experience that people must have to do a job. Competency also includes the idea of confidence. People are not fully competent until they have the confidence to use their knowledge, skill, and experience.

The Springfield Re-manufacturing Company (SRC) was featured on February 7, 1990, on *The McNeil/Lehrer Report*. Jack Stack, the president of SRC, reported a remarkable turnaround in the company, which overhauls old truck engines. So remarkable was the turnaround that Mercedes now sends its engines from Germany to SRC for overhaul rather than having them done in Germany. Sales have tripled in six years.

Not only has SRC developed all its work units into superior work teams, it has turned the whole organization into a superior work team. Using what it calls The Game of Business, it models itself after the typical American baseball or football team. The game has three rules:

1. Know the rules.
2. Learn to read the scores.
3. Have a stake in the game.

These rules have given SRC a structure for making full use of the human resources of its teams. Here are a few examples.

Under rule one, everyone in the work team is expected to know how to do everyone else's job. Because each team member has this greater competency, the typical cycle of too much work and too little work is eliminated. When one team member has a period of slack in his or her own job, that team member immediately starts working with a fellow team member who has a backlog.

Under rule two, every person is taught how to read the company's financial reports and to know what implications the numbers have for profit and loss. Every person in SRC knows how the company makes money, if the company is making money, and exactly how his or her job is influencing these outcomes.

Under rule three, the employees and managers own the company. All decisions that affect the company are made by employees and managers. A considerable growth in competency is required of most people to become expert business people.

Recently, SRC had to decide whether to pay out a bonus or to use the extra cash to liquidate the company's debt, thereby making the stock more valuable. The employees voted not to take the bonus.

Superior work teams make the most of their people, and they are always on a learning curve. They don't learn a job—they learn the team's whole business, whatever it is. No work processes "hiccup" because a key member happens to be absent. Their jobs are what they do, but the team is what they own. Members feel fully responsible for everything that happens in their team. As one rate clerk put it:

> You were expected to know your job and the rest of the jobs in
> the office as well. About the worst thing that you could do was

to tell a customer to call back because there was no one in the office who could answer a question or compute the correct shipping rate.

As a result of attending one of my TQM seminars, a mechanical engineering design team of EG&G Florida greatly expanded its use of the competencies of its drafters. Before making these changes in the way the drafters worked, engineers dictated work assignments. The workload fluctuated between too much work, with large backlogs, and too little work, with the drafters sitting around waiting for their next assignments. The drafters did only drafting. They had a very limited opportunity to learn new knowledge and skills, and the result was boredom and low morale. Since only the engineers could set priorities, there were periods of a large backlog. Engineers could take the drafters off one job and put them on another. The drafters were forced to be less productive than they might have been because they lost so much time stopping one job, gearing up for a new job, stopping that job and gearing up for another job.

The current state of affairs, by contrast, is that drafters and engineers now review projects together from the moment of inception. Drafters now research the system documentation required before each new project. They collect the floor plans from facility books, get the appropriate system drawings, and the like. Drafters do field research along with the engineers and collaborate with the engineers in visualizing the total requirements of the new project. They perform the technical assessment of new projects with the engineers and develop cost estimates. And drafters perform verification of as-built conditions—that is, verify that the project was built to specifications and close out the required documentation.

The quantity and quality of the output of this team has greatly improved since it began to make better use of the resource it has in its drafters. This improvement has been acknowledged by the company, and the team has received many team awards in the past year for its performance.

Because of this success, plans are now under way for drafters to begin to do all the work on small designs—from conceptualization, to researching the documentation, to drawing the design, to as-built verification.

Strategic Considerations in Maximizing Use of Human Resources

Superior work teams make full use of the competencies that members already possess, and they give members the opportunity to gain new competencies. When teams begin to target opportunities for improving their use of their human resources, they do well to keep in mind a number of special considerations. These considerations can help them both identify opportunities for improvement and select the best strategies for undertaking these improvements.

- Competencies beget competencies; that is, the more competencies that team members have a chance to use, the more competencies they will develop.

- Competencies of members can be expanded either in an outward direction or horizontally.

- Competencies of members can be expanded in a downward direction or vertically.

- In addition to their technical and job competencies, members must have special competencies in order to function successfully as team members.

Competencies Beget Competencies

The potential that the human resources represent in a team is made up of its individual and collective competencies. The use of competencies is cumulative. The more use that is made of competencies, the more competent people become. The more competent people become, the more competencies they want to gain. As people gain new competencies, they want to use these competencies. The more they use these new competencies, the more competent they become, and so the spiral continues.

Competencies can be physical—ones that require psychomotor dexterity or strength. We cannot expect, however, any significant improvement in the performance of most teams by getting people to lift or carry more. We cannot, in fact, expect any significant improvement in America's competitive position by getting people to work harder physically. We will make significant gains only by making better and fuller use of people's minds.

People are naturally disposed to demonstrate their competencies. Given half a chance, people will use more and more of their competencies to achieve the goals of their teams. Because of this, all that is typically required to get people to demonstrate their competencies in a work team is to give them the chance. We have examples on every hand of workers going out of their way to apply their competencies—even fighting management and other barriers to do so.

The first consideration that should guide our selection of strategies for expanding the use of a team's human resources is that competencies beget competencies. All teams really have to do is get started, take the lid off, and start almost anywhere. It is difficult to imagine any strategy that is designed to take fuller advantage of people's competencies failing. It is only a matter of letting people become what they want to be—more and more competent.

One caution should be made: never begin to make fuller use of people's competencies unless you intend to permit the process to continue. To start to encourage the use and growth of competency and then to shut these processes down will have a deadly impact on team performance.

One software design team took a sharp downward turn in its performance after it changed team leaders. The first leader had done such things as involving all members in the design of each new project, assigning each new team member a mentor, and holding regular seminars led by team members on some aspect of their work or on some new technology development. But the new team leader fancied himself an authority on all aspects of the team's work, stopped involving all members in projects design, and eliminated most of the other strategies his predecessor had used to use team members' competencies. One clear indicator of the new leader's impact was that, within a year, most team members had transferred out of the unit and the others were in the process of doing so.

The condition of this team was worse after opportunities to be competent were shut off than it had been before these opportunities were started.

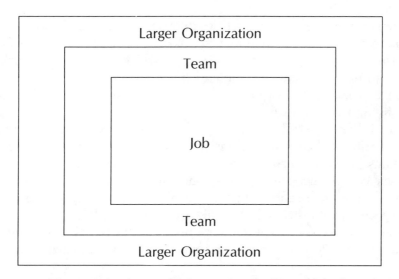

Figure 4–1. *Arenas for Improving the Use of People*

When teams consider extending the use of people's competencies, they can operate on the assumption that people want to demonstrate their competencies. People will, with rare exceptions, respond positively to any chance to show what they know and what they can do. Teams can make the most of their human resources by identifying and considering opportunities in two dimensions: a horizontal dimension and a vertical dimension:

Horizontal Opportunities

First of all, opportunities to make more use of the human resources can be visualized starting with a person's job and then extending outward into the team and into the larger organization. These opportunities might be thought of as three overlapping rectangles. The inner rectangle is a person's job, the next rectangle out is the team, and the third one out is the larger organization (figure 4–1).

Job designs that require that jobholders perform a predetermined set of tasks and only those tasks most severely restrict people's influence. Designs that are less restrictive encourage people to apply more of their competencies to their jobs in several ways. People are encouraged to find new tasks, to eliminate unnecessary tasks, and to improve the processes by which they do their work.

Job-enlargement and job-enrichment practices typically focus on expanding the use of people's competencies in their assigned jobs. Superior work teams encourage their members to enlarge and enrich their jobs. They encourage people to apply all of their competencies to their jobs—its tasks and its processes. Superior work teams, however, also do a lot more. They expect people to apply their competencies in areas beyond the job—to the team and to the larger organization. In traditional organizations, workers are expected to do their jobs the best that they can. In superior work teams, workers are expected not only to do their jobs in a superior fashion, but to make their teams and their whole organizations superior.

A second strategic consideration for teams to keep in mind is to take advantage of the opportunities in each person's job in the team and beyond the team, in the larger organization. A third consideration is to take advantage of vertical opportunities.

Vertical Opportunities

Vertical opportunities are a function of the demand made on people's minds in at least four levels. The first level is giving information. The second level is developing and communicating new ideas. The third level is making decisions. The final and fourth level is solving problems.

These levels suggest an increasing level of complexity and difficulty. But creating a new idea may be more complex than making a decision. It is best to think of these different levels as different opportunities for using competencies and different opportunities for learning new competencies. These levels overlap and rarely exist in a pure state. To solve a problem typically requires that people give information. It may require new ideas. It most often will require making a decision.

The horizontal and vertical dimensions of team competency are displayed the Competencies and Involvement Grid (figure 4–2).

Activity \ Area	Job	Team	Larger Organization
Information			
New Ideas			
Decisions			
Solving Problems			

Figure 4–2. *Competencies and Influence Grid*

The grid provides a logical way to plan and implement strategies for making maximum use of a team's human resources.

Thus, three important considerations should be kept in mind as teams explore possibilities for making a fuller use of their human resources.

- The more people use their competencies, the more competencies they develop.

- Opportunities exist to extend the use of people's competencies beyond their jobs to their teams and to the larger organization, in an outward direction.

- Opportunities exist to extend the use of people's competencies in a vertical direction, from giving information to solving problems.

A final consideration that teams should keep in mind is that superior work teams require people to have the skill to function as team members.

Special Competencies for Being Team Members

Teams are able to make the maximum use of their human resources when they develop two key understandings about the potential of their members.

1. Members will develop and use more competencies as members of a superior work team than they will by themselves.

2. The team's competency is a great deal more than the sum of the competencies of its individual members.

People can be more competent in a team environment than on their own, and a team's total competency can greatly exceed the collective competency of its members. On superior work teams people are in touch with one another and interact freely. They share their competencies with each other. Ideas from one person are built on and improved by others. Insights from one member stimulate new insights from others. Members teach each other. These highly dynamic processes of sharing information, learning from each other, challenging each other, and teaching each other create a special environment for making the very best use of a team's human resources. For teams to create this special environment, team members must develop the following kinds of competencies:

- rational problem-solving skills
- interpersonal problem-solving skills, and
- team meeting effectiveness skills.

Rational Problem-Solving Skills. These skills help team members conduct efficient and effective problem-solving discussions and meetings by building structures for developing information, analyzing information, identifying alternative strategies, and making decisions. These structures affect competencies by increasing the use made of individual team-member competencies, and adding new competencies through increased synergism.

Structured problem-solving environments increase the possibility that all the human resources in a team will be used. In unstructured environments, input is often determined by the relative position and authority that people have, or by the personal relationships that exist on the team, or by just how aggressive or self-confident a team member might be. Structure can create clarity about direction and process. The result is to increase the comfort level of team members and to free them up to participate more actively.

Structured problem solving also increases team competency because structure makes it easier for team members to build on what others contribute, and structure keeps developing ideas from being lost. When teams interact in a random and unstructured way, a lot of information and new ideas can just "fall through the cracks" and go uncaptured and unremembered.

Structured problem solving also makes it easier for team members to develop new competencies. Problem-solving structures can give order to the synergistic quality of a team's interactions. Synergism is a process in which ideas trigger new ideas, insights trigger new insights, and opportunities trigger new opportunities. Synergism is the increase in total knowledge, skill, and wisdom that can take place through the interaction of team members. The new knowledge, skill, and insight produced through synergism become the property of all the team members. In typical outcomes produced through synergism, everyone has learned something new.

The appendix describes brainstorming and the nominal group technique, tools for rational problem solving.

Interpersonal Problem-Solving Skills. A second necessary set of special team competencies is interpersonal problem-solving skills. These skills underlie the ability of team members to interact in ways that maximize their ability to perform all their team-development and team-performance tasks while maintaining positive relationships with one another. I have discussed at some length the processes and skills associated with successful interpersonal problem-solving communication in an earlier book (Kinlaw 1989).

To make the most of a team's potential, members must have the interpersonal competency to create conversations with each other that have two key characteristics: respect and mutuality (Kinlaw 1989).

Respect. Respect is a function of the amount of information that is developed among team members, and of the ease with which this information is developed. Team members feel respected when they feel other team members listen to them and encourage them to give information and to offer ideas. They do not feel respected when their ideas are rejected without a fair hearing, when they are ridiculed, or when they are patronized.

Mutuality. The most successful conversations are mutual—that is, reciprocal or balanced. Team members involve each other fully in the communication process. The best problem-solving conversations are ones of mutual exploration and discovery. They are built on team members' recognition that each brings something special to each conversation. One team member knows some things, and others know different things. One member will look at a problem from one perspective, and others will have different perspectives. Good problem-solving conversations make the most out of the diversity that team members represent.

Teams require special skills to make the most of the resource that their members represent. Besides rational problem-solving skills and interpersonal problem-solving skills, they need an ability to function as value-added participants in team meetings.

Team Meeting Effectiveness Skills. Team meetings are integral to the development of teams into superior work teams. Team meetings are required for the ongoing processes of sharing information and ideas, of setting goals, of making decisions, of solving problems, and of introducing and managing change. More and more, jobholders will be members of several teams at the same time. They will be members of their own permanent work team, as well as members of a variety of temporary teams and special focus teams like productivity teams, interface teams, tiger teams, action teams, and the like. Team members require the skills to organize team meetings and to function as team members and leaders during team meetings.

I will not give here a detailed description of the various skills that are required to make team meetings effective and efficient. A number of useful books have already been published on this subject (Boreman and Boreman 1972; Bradford 1976). A detailed description of my Team Meeting Effectiveness Model is included as a Key Strategy in chapter 8.

The first Result identified in the model that superior work teams achieve is maximum use of the team's human resources. Teams should keep a number of considerations in mind as they concentrate on making more and more use of their human resources.

In the following section I will discuss the second Result that superior work teams characteristically achieve—superior outputs against all odds.

Superior Output against All Odds

Output includes all the team's services and products that will be used by a customer. A customer may be a person or a group. All teams have internal customers; some teams serve external customers as well. Superior work teams deliver superior outputs to all their customers. An Air Force technician in a missile group describes an averted catastrophe.

> We had a false alert, and the missiles were automatically armed with nuclear warheads. The silos were open. How we ever got all the cooperation that we needed in the time we had, I'll never know. It was just one of those things. We knew we had to do it. It was impossible to think of failure and the consequences.

A test conductor for an aerospace manufacturing group remembers the following experience on her test team.

> We were told at the time that there was no overtime left. We were at the safety limits that the company had established. But we all knew that we had to make the schedule. Not to make the schedule was unthinkable. So we just shut the doors, and everyone worked for free. And it was like no one even had to say that was what we were going to do. Somebody just shut the doors, and we kept working.

A supervisor in a project group describes his team's refusal to accept any problem as unsolvable.

We had a word for getting things done in spite of every possible screwup. The word was *workarounds*. At every status review, if anyone had a problem, no body left the table until we had figured out a satisfactory workaround.

Other typical comments that have been made to me are:

- "We all worked very hard, there wasn't much slack, we were on a tight schedule."

- "We never gave up, we always found a way to keep moving ahead in spite of the obstacles, to solve problems, to fix things."

- "We simply did a superior job and outperformed everybody's expectations."

- "We just did more than any one thought we could. I think that most of us—way down deep in our hearts—had plenty of doubt. But no one dared talk gloom and doom. I think the group would have lynched anybody who did."

None of the people who describe their best teams have ever suggested that these teams were able to do "satisfactory work" because they had all the time, money, and people they needed. Most people mention some set of circumstances that made their achievement particularly difficult.

The best teams that people seem to remember most readily are teams that did something special—performed in a particularly outstanding way. More striking than their superior performance or achievement is that it was gained over, through, and around all sorts of obstacles and unexpected events. The best teams often push their resources and their people to the limits.

Based on the way that people describe their superior work teams, I have come to accept a couple of things about these teams and the obstacles they overcome.

First, superior work teams have a way of just naturally creating obstacles. They tend to commit themselves to goals that often border on the impossible. Second, they sometimes become so intense and focused in going after their "impossible" goals that they may create a good bit of resistance from people who can't change and who don't know how to get out of the way.

There is apparently an interactive effect between being a superior work team and achieving superior result. It is impossible to know which happens first or which causes the other. But achieving superior output is always a hallmark of superior teamwork and superior work teams.

This point may seem simplistic, self-evident, redundant, or tautological. I seem to be defining a superior work team as a superior work team. But it is not quite as obvious or simple as it may seem.

I have asked hundreds of people to talk to me about their best teams. They can talk about teams in which everyone was friendly, or ones in which they enjoyed themselves, or ones in which there was a relaxed atmosphere. A few people do mention such teams. But they are very few. The most typical responses to the open-ended question, "Tell me about your best work team," are the kinds of statements that I have included throughout this book. It has been a rare experience for me that when given the chance to talk about their best teams, people don't talk about some very special kinds of achievement.

Several important insights can be drawn from this connection of superior performance and superior teams that can be used to evolve and select strategies for challenging teams to new levels of superior performance.

Strategic Considerations for Superior Output

In developing strategies that focus on superior output as an opportunity to improve team development and performance, it is quite useful to keep in mind some of the factors that have significant impact on achieving this Result. These factors are:

- Superior outputs against all odds can be achieved only when people are fully **committed** to the team's goals and values.

- People become fully committed to a team's goals and values when these goals and values are clear, have **meaning,** and reflect something over which they have some influence.

- A team, when given a chance, will set **higher output goals** for itself than those set by an external authority.

Commitment

I have discussed at some length the nature and meaning of commitment in a earlier book (Kinlaw, 1989). One thing is quite clear about sustained superior output: it can be attained only through individuals who are fully committed to the team's goals and values.

A team of technicians at a shipyard was trying to evacuate a drum in an engine room of a ship in the yard. The drum contained lubrication oil. It was so placed in the engine room that the team was unable to pump out the oil. None of the pumps or other equipment that were customarily used on such jobs would work.

In shipyards, repair and overhaul schedules are important and tight. Delays can be extremely costly and very damaging to a yard's reputation. Every aspect of repair and overhaul work is typically interrelated. There is always a ripple effect in problems and delays.

This team was very aware that in this particular ship's repair schedule, they had just so much time to evacuate the lubricating oil drum. They were at an impasse, and the pressure was beginning to mount. Then one technician suggested that he thought he could do the job with a small pump that he used to extract oil from the diesel engine in his boat by going through the dipstick port. So without asking permission from anyone, he literally ran to his car and drove home through midday commercial traffic to get the pump. He returned with the pump, and it worked. The ship's repair was completed on time, thousands of dollars were saved, and the yard added a bit more luster to its reputation.

The technician clearly did not have to do what he did. No one knew in advance that the special problem with the oil drum would come up. No one could know that the technician had a pump that just might work. No one would have been the wiser if the technician had not gotten his pump and saved the day. No one could have ordered the technician to go get his pump. Saving the job and completing the ship's repair on time had had absolutely nothing to do with control. It had had to do with the technicians's intense commitment. Like his fellow team members, he thought first of the team's goals. Everything he did naturally followed from that commitment. What the technician did was a knee-jerk reaction. It probably never occurred to him not to go get his pump.

Sustained superior output cannot be achieved through the traditional processes of control. Superior sustained output occurs when people want it and when they work in environments that support them in achieving it. The determination of a work team to be a *superior* work team is totally under the control of the team. People have to decide to be superior—they cannot be controlled or coerced into being superior. The notion that output can be controlled is a bankrupt concept that continues to confound many attempts to improve quality and regain a competitive edge. Managing and organizing work with the expectation that superior output can be controlled is a false hope for the following reasons:

- Workers typically know more about their jobs than do their supervisors.

- The most important contributions that workers make is not in doing what can be predicted (that is, controlled) but in responding to the unexpected (that is, what can't be controlled).

- Much of what workers decide to do or not to do goes unnoticed by their supervisors.

The first factor that has considerable impact on a team's total output is the degree of commitment of the team's members. The alternative to commitment—control—is not a truly viable one. A second factor is the degree of influence team members have in creating meaningful goals and values.

Clear, Meaningful Goals and Values that Team Members Influence

A consistent finding of myself and other researchers is that work teams that have clarity about their goals and values (that they perceive as meaningful) will consistently outperform teams that do not (Hackman 1978; Kinlaw 1983, 1988; Locke 1981; Varney, 1989). We can perceive a hierarchy in the impact that goals and values have on output. Clarity alone about goals and values will have a positive impact on performance (Bulker 1986). When goals and values are not only clear but perceived as being meaningful, they will have an even stronger impact on output. The full impact of goals and values is realized when team members influence what these goals and values are.

When workers are involved in setting team goals and values, they help to ensure that these goals and values are clear and meaningful them. But influence also creates a sense of ownership, which in turn helps generate the sense of commitment that is so essential to sustained superior output.

A second factor that has great potential to move a team toward sustained superior output is the degree to which its clear, meaningful goals and values are created by the team itself. A third factor is the tendency of teams—when given the chance—to set very high goals for themselves.

Teams Have Higher Output Goals When They Set Them

When work teams began to set production goals at a General Electric plant, they set their goals 50 percent higher than they had been before they had any substantial influence in setting their goals (Sherwood 1988).

A few years ago I consulted with a wind-tunnel test team to establish output measures. My first step was to get the team to identify its key results, to set measures to track these results, and to accept responsibility for these results. One key result that the team identified was technical papers. When I started working with the team, it averaged eight papers a year. After the team became involved in measuring its results, it voluntarily set a goal to more than double its old output: twenty technical papers per year.

A few months ago, members of a printing branch attended a TQM seminar of mine. During the seminar these team members decided to review the goals that management had set for them for production and quality. One of the several goals that this team set for itself was to halve the error rate currently targeted for them by management. Within six months they achieved this goal that they had voluntarily set and that greatly exceeded anything management felt possible.

The second result that superior work teams typically achieve is superior output against all odds. Focusing on output is a major vehicle for developing superior work teams. In selecting strategies to improve output, the following considerations should be kept in mind:

- Superior output against all odds can be achieved only when people are fully committed to the team's goals and values.

- People become fully committed to a team's goals and values when these goals and values are clear, have meaning, and reflect something over which they have some influence.

- A team, when given a chance, will set higher output goals for itself than those set by some external authority.

The third Result identified in the Model for Superior Team Development and Performance is continuous improvement. I turn next to this Result and describe more fully what it means, and I outline a few strategic considerations that should be kept in mind as teams select strategies for focusing on this opportunity.

Continuous Improvement

Continuous improvement is a difficult idea for American jobholders to understand. My experience in presenting the idea to hundreds of managers and employees in various TQM seminars and team-development programs over the years is that most participants respond to the idea of continuous improvement with a good bit of hostility. There are a number of reasons for this.

First, an expectation of continuous improvement is not built into the culture of most organizations. You will not find continuous improvement in job descriptions, and you will not find continuous improvement as a priority among managers. It is not that people are against continuous improvement; it is just that they have difficulty becoming true zealots for improvement because their businesses and unions have been so successful in conditioning them

- to do their jobs the way they were set up when they took their jobs;

- to believe that improvement is not their business, but the business of management or somebody "up there";

- to believe that they are already doing about all they can do and don't have time to worry about improvements;

- to have little commitment to improvement because they don't believe they will realize any real benefit from it; and

- to resist any change as disruptive—including improvement.

In addition to these conditioning factors, other reasons keep work units from committing themselves to continuous improvement. First, continuous improvement is not a clear, unambiguous organizational value that is fully supported and fully rewarded; and second, people often do not have the tools for continuous improvement.

Continuous improvement is a Result that takes time to achieve. For work units to improve everything they do, they must have the time to identify opportunities, to take action, and to test alternatives. It is difficult for work units to develop themselves into teams and to improve their total performance if they have not received some sort of permission. That permission is a cornerstone to the success of TQM. It is TQM, more than any other single program or initiative, that is causing organizations to accept continuous improvement as a fundamental condition for their survival. One of my favorite improvement mottos is, "If you ain't getting better, you're getting worse."

The key to continuous improvement is teamwork and team development. Teams create possibilities for improvement that are simply not possible in work units that are managed by control and that depend largely on individual effort.

Opportunities for improvement are everywhere. One clear area is the area of rework and repair. Joseph Juran, an internationally renowned quality expert, claims that a third of what we do consists of redoing what was done before (*TQM Message* 1989). But opportunities also exist in every work process, in every supply action, in response times, and in every repair cycle. Opportunities exist in every aspect of a team's development and performance.

Teams are synonymous with improvement. It is through teams that most of the important improvements in the performance of organizations are taking place. There can now be no question that teams are the major source of improvements like

- improved quality in service and products;
- reduction of absenteeism and turnovers;
- cost reductions in materials and manpower; and
- the commitment of continuous improvement.

A follow-up process used for all teams attending my TQM seminar helps track just what results the seminar achieves. The seminar draws teams from NASA and from six aerospace contractor groups at NASA's Kennedy Space Center. Here are just a few of the improvements achieved by a sample of the three hundred teams that have attended the seminar:

- computerized project tracking reports that have increased accuracy and reduced time in monitoring projects and reporting their status;

- a 50 percent reduction of space required for storage of materials;

- a significant reduction of unsafe tools;

- cross training in many different groups, such as a systems configuration management team, a procurement office, a design engineering branch, and a security control group;

- team management of overtime roster and shift schedule;

- the use of work-flow diagrams to teach new team members their jobs;

- development of baseline performance data by team surveys; and

- regularized update and feedback sessions with customers.

The fourth largest investor-owned electric utility in the United States, Florida Power and Light (FPL) has more than three million customers and eighteen thousand employees. As I noted earlier, FPL was the first recipient of the Deming Prize, a prestigious Japanese recognition for world-class quality. FPL is organized into seventeen hundred quality teams. The Deming Prize citation for FPL noted such improvements as:

- a reduction of lost-time injuries from more than one per hundred employees to 0.42 per hundred;

- a reduction of customer complaints to the lowest level in ten years; and

- the reduction of customer service interruptions from one hundred minutes in 1982 to forty-eight minutes in 1989.

It is inconceivable that these Results at FPL could have been made by any other means than teamwork. There is no other known way of harnessing the human and technical potential of an organization for such a level of sustained improvement in performance.

Strategic Considerations for Continuos Improvement

Teams should keep in mind at least two guidelines or considerations in order to make continuous improvement a routine part of a team's achievements.

- A **systemic approach** should be taken.

- Continuous improvement should be viewed as a **long-term, incremental process,** not as a quick fix.

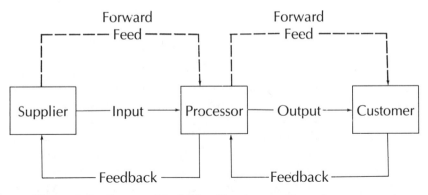

Figure 4–3. *Systems Model for Continuous Team Improvement*

A Systemic Approach to Continuous Improvement

Figure 4–3 is a simple systems model of any team or team member that produces products or services for a customer. I have included the model in chapter 8 as a Key Strategy and will discuss it at length there.

The Systems Model for Continuous Team Improvement can be used to analyze both the performance of individual team members and total team performance. Each individual on a team is sometimes a Supplier, sometimes a Processor, and sometimes a Customer. Team members are continuously receiving inputs from other team members, processing these inputs, and passing outputs to other team members. Work teams function the same way. They also have the three roles of Supplier, Processor, and Customer. Since my subject is team development and performance, I will not be discussing the roles of individual team members.

The systems model helps a team do two things relative to continuous improvement. First, it stimulates a work team to think of itself in its three roles of Supplier, Processor, and Customer and to consider the multitude of opportunities for improvement in these three roles. Second, the model helps a team visualize the interrelatedness of improvement initiatives and consider how an improvement in one element of the system might also improve other elements in the system.

Long Term and Incremental

The important improvements in a team's development and performance will take place over the long term. Most likely, these improvements will be slow and not immediately apparent. One of the major hurdles that teams (and whole organizations) face as they begin their journey toward continuous improvement is the temptation to look for the quick fix.

Recently, I helped a large and traditionally managed organization begin to plan for a quality management initiative that it had decided to undertake. At the very first session with the TQM staff, the issue of payoffs and results became the number one issue. The newly formed TQM staff was convinced that if they could not show some immediate and rather impressive results, the program would never receive the support that it required from the organization's senior officials. So the staff initially spent a good bit of time looking for targets of opportunity to obtain a short-term return rather than working the long-term problems of organizational values, management style, alienation, and distrust in the work force, lack of quality management processes, and the like.

If a team looks for short-term, immediate payoffs from its improvement initiatives, it will have the same experience that people have who try to lose weight with "miracle" diets rather than through the long and tedious process of changing their whole lifestyle. The pattern of the quick fix is predictable.

In the first stage of a quick fix, the team throws itself into an improvement project with some enthusiasm. In the second stage, it experiences some apparent success—even a little euphoria. In the third stage, it recognizes that its improvements are retrogressing or that new improvement targets are getting harder to identify. In the fourth stage, the team becomes disillusioned, and the improvement process falls apart. In the final stage, the team returns to business as usual.

The rise and fall of quality circles in many organizations has followed a pattern like this. After starting with a good bit of fanfare and ritual, a team falters under the burden of showing immediate results. It looks for easy problems and quick fixes. It loses what little management support it had at the beginning. It finds itself using its meetings in "trivial pursuits," and soon members stop coming to meetings and the circle falls apart.

Summary

This chapter has described in detail the Results that superior teams achieve: maximum use of its human resources, superior outputs against all odds, and continuous improvement. It has also discussed some strategic considerations that should guide teams to improve their Results.

The three strategic considerations that are related to these Results are summarized below.

Maximizing the Team's Human Resources

Teams should keep in mind the following considerations when they focus on improving the use of their human resources:

- The more competencies that team members have a chance to use, the more competencies they will want to use; that is, competencies beget competencies.

- They can expand the use of competencies in an outward or horizontal direction.

- They can expand the use of competencies in a vertical or downward direction.

- There are special team member competencies that must be developed and used.

Superior Outputs against All Odds

Teams can best improve output if they are aware that

- Superior outputs against all odds can be achieved only when people are fully *committed* to the team's goals and values.

- People become fully committed to a team's goals and values when these goals and values are *clear, have meaning,* and reflect something over which they had some *influence.*

- People, when given a chance, will set *higher output goals* for themselves than those set by some external authority.

Continuous Improvement

Teams can best affect continuous improvement if they take

- a systemic approach, and

- view continuous improvement as a long-term and incremental process.

In the next chapter I will describe in some detail the next primary element in the Model for Superior Team Development and Performance, the Informal Processes characteristic of superior work teams.

5
Focusing on Informal Team Processes

The Model for Superior Team Development and Performance has four primary elements: Results, Informal Processes, Feelings, and Leadership. In chapter 4, I discussed Results and outlined some strategic considerations for improving each of the three subelements included in that category.

The second primary element in the model is Informal Processes. In chapter 3, I gave an overview of the Informal Processes that superior work teams create and employ. In this chapter, I will

- describe in greater detail the Informal Processes; and

- discuss some strategic considerations that should be taken into account when teams set out to improve their Informal Processes.

Superior work teams (and work units that periodically rise to the level of superior teamwork) typically develop and use at least four Informal Processes.

- communicating and contacting
- responding and adapting
- influencing and improving, and
- appreciating and celebrating.

Superior-work-team members described their teams as places of fluid interaction and easy conversation. They talk about the many different informal acts and behaviors of team members that turned their units into teams that pulsed with life and energy.

As a member of a launch test team describes her experience:

> I felt really "up" at work. In fact, I felt excited just thinking about what we were doing and the people I was working with. One of the things I remember the clearest was that everybody's job was everybody's job. We all looked to each other to get the whole job done. I don't remember anyone ever saying they were too busy to help me, and I don't remember ever being surprised about some change or the impact of some delay or things like that.
>
> Most of all, I remember feeling that no one was going to leave me alone with my problems. Come to think of it, we never thought much about who had what problem—just how to fix the damn thing.

A division in a large East Coast company with which I have consulted has a number of the characteristics that I associate with superior work teams. The manager of that division has spoken on several occasions about his own organizational philosophy. He describes his division this way:

> I consider organizational charts and job descriptions what we use to explain to outsiders who we are and what we do. But there isn't much about those wire diagrams that describes how we actually work together. My experience is that we have built our excellent reputation because no one stays in those little neat rectangles that we draw on the charts.
>
> I sure don't want people wondering if it's their job before they take action or fix a problem. I like the story of the little boy who saw a hole in the dike, stuck his finger in the hole, and kept it there all night until he was relieved and engineers showed up to fix it. You can just imagine how things would have gone if the boy had started reporting the problem through channels and the city fathers had called a special meeting to investigate the boy's report. By morning, the whole town would have been adrift in the Zuider Zee.

It is important to keep in mind two qualities of Informal Processes. First, they are informal. Second, they are so interrelated that they are often all going on at the same time in a single conversation between team members or in a single action of the team.

I have called the four key processes in the Model for Superior Team Development and Performance "informal" to distinguish them clearly from the formal systems that organizations and work units use to structure and control their work. No one must obtain permission to use Informal Processes. They are not governed by rules and regulations. You will not find them described in an organization's policies and practices manual. They don't follow any predictable pattern. No one is told when and when not to use them. No team training programs directly address them. These Informal Processes are part of the day-to-day work of superior work teams. They reflect the norms that the team has established and that members instinctively follow.

The processes are not only informal but very interrelated and interdependent.

When team members are in easy touch and when communication is open and free, they are typically responding and adapting to some issue or problem and influencing some outcome. The routine process of showing appreciation is possible only when people are in contact and know at first hand what their peers are doing and contributing.

The first Informal Process characteristic of superior work teams is **communicating and contacting.**

Communicating and Contacting

Superior-work-team members are informal in the way they communicate and interact. You would have difficulty discovering their titles and levels of authority by how they dress. Their conversations are free of pretense and self-serving nonsense. People have status through their work and their ideas, not through something as silly as dress or position. Informality gives rise to a good bit of humor and friendly banter. It is typical on superior work teams for everyone to use first names. It is also typical for members to have immediate and easy access to each other and to their supervisors. This does not mean, of course, that superior work teams are social clubs. Communicating and contacting are focused on getting the job done.

The kinds of remarks that I have recorded from people who described the process of communicating and contacting are:

- "Nobody stood on ceremony. From the project manager right down to the people who swept the shop floors, everybody used first names. We had people with all kinds of titles and degrees, but you couldn't tell who was leading and who was following from the way we talked and acted."

- "If you needed to see anybody about anything, you didn't go through channels or get permission. You just went and talked to the person that had the information you wanted or the expertise to help you."

- "Our supervisor was everywhere. He knew exactly what was going on all the time. No matter what kind of problem you had, he seemed to already know about it. It really made a big difference not to have to explain over and over again what I was doing and the kinds of roadblocks I kept running into."

- "Before we got started really trying to be a team, we never got any information about what other people were doing or what was happening that would affect us. We were all treated like mushrooms. But we really turned things around when we started doing things like having regular crew meetings and status meetings. Everything got better. We got to know each other better and we started helping each other a lot more. Before I got transferred it was the best team I've ever worked on."

Strategic Considerations for Improving Communication and Contact

When teams begin to focus on improving the Informal Process of communicating and contacting, they should keep in mind two issues or conditions that influence its development and successful use.

- Never underestimate the difficulty in creating free, open, easy communication and contact in a team. Informal communicating and contacting are often not the norm in work units, and there may be considerable **resistance** to such a process.

- The Process of communicating and contacting can impact on a team's performance only when it is a **quality process**—that is, when people have the requisite interpersonal communication skills.

Resistances to Informal Communicating and Contacting

In my experience, one great inhibitor to team effectiveness is the fear and distrust that people have of informal communicating and contacting.

I recently made a presentation to a senior management team. During my presentation the senior official was present with members of her staff. Throughout the presentation, no one spoke or responded to what I had to say except the senior official. I would make a statement, then the senior official would nod agreement or express an exception using some tired aphorism or irrelevancy like, "There's nothing new about that," or "We still have too many people who don't want to work," or, "The manager's job is to tell people what to do and then see that they do it." Try as I might, I could get none of her staff to become involved in the conversation. The senior official was making important decisions that would affect the whole organization, but not one member of her staff was prepared to risk an opinion. I was hardly surprised when I later overheard one senior manager say to his deputy, "If you ever take a staff meeting for me, don't you ever tell her about any problems we are having."

Candor is built upon frequent informal conversations in which the risk of being truthful is tested over and over again. Teams and organizations pay an enormous price in productivity and quality when people are afraid to give their opinions, offer alternatives, admit to problems, and offer new ideas.

One of the less insightful questions that I am sometimes asked is, "Don't you think that it is possible for people to communicate too much and that people can have too much information?" What lies behind this question is various myths and misconceptions like these:

- "If you give people too much information, it will only upset them or make them worry." (This kind of thinking suggests the myth that it is better not to tell a patient that he or she is going to die so the patient won't get upset.)

- "People need to concentrate on their jobs and not about what is going on around them." (It is just this kind of wrong thinking that has been a major inhibitor to team development and improved organizational performance.)

- "If I level with other people, they might just start leveling with me." (Of course, it is precisely the large number of unexamined ideas, decisions, and management practices that have taken us out of the competitive race.)

- "If people really want to know something, it's their job to find out."

One of the great inhibitors of efficient and effective work is that people feel obliged to figure out what it is safe to say. We have only the slightest notion of the amount of wasted effort and time that go into the business of people figuring out what they can tell their bosses and peers or even what questions are safe to ask.

Every time I run a seminar for managers, I get an awful lot of questions like these:

- "How can you help your boss make a good decision when he has already made up his mind and really isn't prepared to look at any more alternatives?"

- "How can I tell a peer the real truth and risk hurting his feelings?"

- "How I tell my boss that she is out of touch and really doesn't know what's going on in the shops anymore?"

One way to calibrate just how "career limiting" it can be to give one's unvarnished opinion or to provide timely information (no matter how unwanted it is) is to look at the amount of time organizations devote to training their managers how to negotiate or how to influence others. When people in organizations or work units feel they cannot be candid or speak the truth (as they see it), organizations must spend training budgets in the totally unproductive enterprise of teaching people the totally unproductive behavior of how to become skilled in verbal manipulation.

The first strategic consideration that teams should keep in mind as they consider improving the Informal Process of communicating and contacting is that such improvement can be extremely difficult because truthfulness is often not the norm in most work units and organizations. A second consideration is that to have a positive impact on a team's performance, communication and contact require high levels of interpersonal competency.

Communicating and Contacting Require Skills

Managing by walking around (MBWA) has gained considerable publicity and popularity, as has "staying in touch with the customer," due in large measure to the popularity of In Search of Excellence (Peters and Waterman 1982). Involvement, a related idea, has been made popular through the current emphasis on total quality management. But neither MBWA, nor involvement, nor any other form of informal communicating and contacting will work unless they are quality interactions.

The simple fact is that communicating and contacting can be negative processes as well as positive ones. For some jobholders, having their supervisors walk around is not a useful experience. Too often, what the jobholders get from contact with their bosses and other members of their work units are reprimands, unsolicited feedback, untimely interruptions, and rejection of their ideas.

Often, team members are not very aggressive in getting the opinions of their peers on ideas and plans because of the negative and unhelpful responses they typically receive. Informal communicating and contacting must be a quality process, and quality is a function of skill.

In chapter 4, I briefly discussed interpersonal problem-solving skills in connection with developing various special team competencies. The two key characteristics that I associated with effective problem solving were respect and mutuality. These characteristics apply to any serious conversation. They must characterize all informal communication within teams for communication to have a positive impact on performance.

A number of skills are critical in successful conversations. I have covered these skills in considerable detail in earlier publications and will not repeat that information here (Kinlaw 1981; 1989; 1990). When teams become serious about improving the Informal Process of communicating and contacting, they can consult these or similar resources.

Quality interactions and conversations are characterized not only by respect and mutuality; they also develop useful information.

Team members must have the skill to develop relevant, task-focused information. As they listen and respond to each other, they must be able to focus on plans, actions, events, and data. The desired outcome of all such conversations is developing information, improving understanding, corroborating judgments, verifying data, and the like. To develop relevant information means at least two things:

- creating no barriers to the other person's input; and
- stimulating the other person to input information.

It is particularly difficult for a team member to listen to news that presents problems and issues that he or she isn't expecting or that run counter to his or her perceptions. It is not easy for team members to listen to opinions that force them to devalue their own.

Skilled listening is, of course, the key to developing information successfully. Skilled listening has at least these elements:

1. the ability to receive accurately the whole message sent by another person—that is, the entire verbal, nonverbal and emotional content of a message;

2. the ability to convey to another person by one's own verbal and nonverbal behavior that one is listening; and

3. the ability to encourage another person to continue to speak and build information.

These three elements largely depend on the mental skill to listen nonevaluatively.

Most often, we add our own mental comments to the messages that we receive. We note the degree to which we think what we have heard is true or false, right or wrong, and accurate or inaccurate. When we listen evaluatively, therefore, we are listening very much to ourselves—to our own metal comments as part of the message we are receiving. We are not concentrating on just listening and understanding what the other person is saying. When we listen evaluatively, we tend to act evaluatively and convey judgment or disbelief to the other person—rather than just conveying our understanding.

A second strategic consideration that teams should keep in mind as they plan to improve the Informal Process of communication and contact is that to be successful, this process must be a quality process. To make it a quality process requires that team members have highly developed interpersonal communication skills that permit them to consistently

- convey respect
- maintain mutuality, and
- develop useful information.

These then are two strategic considerations that teams should keep in mind as they consider how to improve the Informal Process of communicating and contacting:

- Never underestimate the difficulty in creating free, open, easy communication and contact in a team. Informal communication and contact are often not the norm in work units, and there may be considerable resistance to such a process.

- Communicating and contacting can impact positively on a team's performance only when it is a quality process—when people have the requisite interpersonal communication skills.

The first Informal Process that is characteristic of superior teams is communicating and contacting. The second is **responding and adapting.**

Responding and Adapting

Superior work teams refuse to be stymied. They view problems as opportunities, and they expect members to take the initiative to respond to problems and issues as they develop. Members join forces easily to respond to changes that affect the whole team. Team members give immediate attention to requests for assistance from one another.

Specific behaviors that are characteristic of superior teams and that illustrate the practical meaning of being responsive and adaptive are that team members

- get immediate help on priority work problems;
- receive serious consideration for suggestions to improve any aspect of the teams's performance;
- have ready access to anyone who can help them get their jobs done;
- receive quick responses from their supervisors to help them resolve personal problems that impact on their work; and
- can get a prompt decision when they need it.

The story of a supervisor in a telephone company illustrates just what responsiveness and adaptability can mean.

We had been told that we would be moving sometime in the near future to a new building that had been built across town. But every time we would get a date, it would change. After a while we just put the whole thing in the back of our minds. In fact, it got to be a kind of joke among the operators. Guys started saying things to each other in the morning like, "Hey, Charlie, you still here? I thought you moved," or, "You want to join our lottery? You have to pick which will come first, the move or your retirement." I can't tell you how many times we packed and unpacked.

Then, it happened. We got the word on a Thursday that we had to move and be up and running on the following Monday. Also, we were told that we couldn't turn off the machines until the end of the working day on Thursday. To be on such a short fuse was bad enough, but just add to that things like we got short-changed on the number of trucks we needed. We had a gate lift break on the back of a truck with a large memory component on it. We got to the new facility and discovered that the electricians hadn't finished their job.

We ended up using some of our own pickups, borrowing some heavy-duty jacks from a house-moving outfit, running our own cables, and doing God only knows what. But when 7:30 rolled around on Monday morning, we were on line. How the hell we did it, I still don't really know. But I can tell you one thing—that was one proud and tired outfit.

Strategic Considerations for Improving Responsiveness and Adaptability

Responsiveness and adaptability are fundamental to superior performance. When teams consider improving this Informal Process, there are at least two considerations that they should remember. First, people often have habits and mindsets that resist the idea of responsiveness. Second, creating high levels of responsiveness and adaptability requires that the process be reinforced over and over again.

Resistances

A staff group recently had the responsibility to take action on data that had been provided from a survey conducted by corporate head-quarters. The survey had taken up a lot of employee time and had

cost a great deal of money. During my work with this staff, I
learned at first hand just how strong the habits of not being responsive and adaptive can become.

I was first commissioned to analyze the study and identify those
of its implications that were unambiguous and that suggested improvement opportunities for the organization. I was told that it was
imperative that I complete my analysis and make a presentation to
this staff group within seven days. My report was delivered on time,
and it was accepted. But the presentation that I was supposed to
give never happened. The staff missed the opportunity to act on the
information from the survey. My later conversations with the group
clearly indicate that no one remembers that there was a need for
quick response. As this is being written, nothing has been done to
use the survey data. What apparently happened was that staff group
initially thought the survey data were important and should be
taken seriously. After I made my analysis, the staff made a presentation to senior management about the survey and what the staff was
doing to act on the findings. Senior management responded negatively to the staff group's presentation. Members of the group re-
acted by dropping its interest in the survey and setting aside the
data. No attempt was made to regroup and find new strategies to
work around the roadblocks that they had encountered with senior
management.

I have conducted hundreds of training programs over the years
in a very wide range of private and public organizations. I have, sad
to say, observed at first hand too often a lack of responsiveness and
adaptability in training offices.

In one training office, each training program was assigned to a
separate coordinator. *Separate* was really the operative word. If I
had even the simplest question about a program, like where it
would be held or on what dates it was scheduled, it was absolutely
impossible to get that information unless the person directly responsible for that program was available. If the person that I needed to
talk to was on leave or sick, I could not get the information. No
one in that training office expected help from a colleague, and no
one asked for help.

Early in my career (before I discovered that to survive I should
never assume that certain clients would take care of even the mini-

mum preparations for a training event), I had several kinds of repetitive experiences.

One repetitive experience goes like this. I arrive at the designated training room thirty minutes before the program is scheduled to start. The door to the training room is locked. Participants are standing in the hall waiting to get in. I try to find a person who has a key. I learn that the person who is responsible for the program will not be in that day. The key is that person's responsibility. No one else on the training staff has any idea how to help, or the inclination to help. I personally find the building superintendent or someone from maintenance and get the door open. I start the program an hour late, and only the participants and myself seem to care.

Another repetitive experience goes like this. I arrive at a training room. The door is open, but the room is a mess. The trash cans are full, tables have not been set up, chairs are stacked, and none of the equipment that was promised by the client is present. I contact my program coordinator. I am told that the room was supposed to have been set up the night before, but another program coordinator had scheduled an evening class, and there had been no time for a cleanup crew to take care of the room. I am also told that the overhead projector was ordered, but for some reason wasn't delivered. As I observe the staff, it is clear that no one else is going to help my program coordinator. No one else feels the slightest responsibility for the group's image or its total performance.

A lack of internal responsiveness in a work unit means that the total performance of the unit suffers. There is no quick or easy way to improve a team's internal responsiveness when habits of not responding have become thoroughly entrenched.

Lack of responsiveness and adaptability have a number of sources.

1. People are told to do their own jobs, and they are held responsible for doing only their own jobs. They never get acknowledged or rewarded for helping someone else. They get fussed at only when they don't do what they have been told to do. Over the years, a myopic focus on one's own job has been rewarded and reinforced.

2. To take any kind of quick action may entail too much risk. People are not sure just how much freedom they have. They worry about breaking a rule or violating a precedent.

3. People in work units may have a strong sense of being in competition with each other. They develop the perception that they can only succeed through the failures of their colleagues.

The resistances to responsiveness may have become part of a work unit's climate. To create high levels of responsiveness and adaptability in such cases requires nothing short of changing the unit's work climate. This means changing the unit's norms. But changing norms never occurs quickly or easily.

The second strategic consideration that affects improving responsiveness and adaptability is that it can usually be done through continuous reinforcement.

Reinforcing the Process

Developing high levels of responsiveness requires continuous attention and reinforcement. One supervisor has developed a set of values in her team that she communicates and discusses with each new person that joins her team. Among the various values that she talks about are the following:

- "Never bring a problem to me unless you have gotten all the help you can from the other team members."

- "Never refuse help to anybody when they ask for it."

- "Never bring a problem to me that you haven't figured out at least three alternative ways to solve."

In another team, at each staff meeting, the first question that is asked is, "Who needs help with anything?" The follow-up question is, "Who can help?"

One highly innovative approach that a team took after attending a seminar of mine was to establish a monthly "slam dunk" award and an "assist" award. The slam dunk award is given to the team member or members who bring the most direct credit to the team by solving a problem or taking care of a special need of a customer. The assist award is given to the member or members who provide the most help to another team member during the month. Any team member can nominate any other team member or members for these awards, and the whole team makes the final decisions.

From the time new employees enter this team, they begin to learn about the importance of responsiveness and adaptability. And the importance of the process is renewed every time an assist award is given out.

Another supervisor in a team that I worked with a few years ago became quite concerned about how often he said no when he was asked for help and the impact that kind of modeling had on the rest of the team. He got the idea of placing two small boxes on his desk. One box was labeled *yes* and the other was labeled *no*. Every time a person asked for assistance and he said yes, he put a green chip in the yes box. Every time he said no, he put a red chip in the no box. He later told me that this technique had put him under much pressure to say yes and had made a big difference in his own responsiveness.

Responsiveness and adaptability is one of the key Informal Processes that support superior-work-team performance. When teams begin to focus on ways to improve this process, there are at least two considerations that they should remember. First, people have often developed habits and mindsets that lead them to resist being responsive and adaptive. Second, creating high levels of responsiveness and adaptability requires that the process be reinforced over and over again.

We have now looked at two informal processes that superior teams employ to support their overall effectiveness: communicating and contacting, and responding and adapting. The next Informal Process that I will examine is *influencing and improving*.

Influencing and Improving

The continuous, incremental improvements that take place in a team are a function of all four Informal Processes. All strengthen the other elements in the Model for Superior Team Development

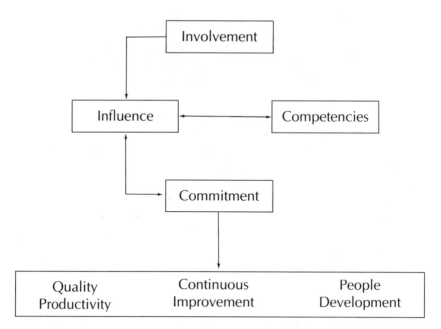

Figure 5–1. *Influence Process and Payoffs*

and Performance. But it is clear that creating opportunities for in-fluence plays a special role in a team's development and perfor-mance because these opportunities are the means of releasing and using the competencies of team members.

In Chapter 4, I discussed how the competencies of a team can be fully used and developed. I introduced the Competencies and Influence Grid (figure 4–2) and showed how it could help teams conceptualize horizontal and vertical opportunities for using and developing the competencies of a team.

The title of the grid explicitly communicates the notion that competencies and influence are inextricably associated. One is nec-essary for the other. For a team to know that a member has a com-petency, the member must demonstrate it. For the member to dem-onstrate a competency, the member must have the opportunity to be influential.

Figure 5–1 gives a graphic display of the relationship between influence, competencies, and payoffs for the team. By extending opportunities for influence, teams tap more and more of the competencies their members have. As competencies are used, members seek more opportunities to be influential. The more opportunities they acquire to be influential, the more competencies they will develop in order to be more influential. And on the process goes. The payoffs from people being influential have now been well documented. The typical results are better quality, better development of people, and continuous improvement (Lawler 1986; Werther 1981).

A few important strategic considerations relate to strengthening team member influence. The first two I have already alluded to in my discussion of competencies in chapter 4—that is, taking advantage of horizontal opportunities and taking advantage of vertical opportunities. These opportunities are clearly apparent in the Competencies and Influence Grid.

There are, however, two additional considerations that teams and organizations should keep in mind when actions to strengthen the influence of people are undertaken.

Strategic Considerations for Strengthening Influence

Three considerations can serve as useful guides in strengthening influence.

- There can be strong **resistances** to extending influence.

- Influence should always be coupled clearly with **improvement.**

- Influencing and improving should be considered as a **way of life** and not as a program.

Resistances

Although extending influence to people has produced demonstrated positive results and although most supervisors believe that strengthening employee influence is a good thing (Klein 1984), there are also a number of deep-seated resistances to extending influence to people. When teams decide to work on the degree of influence that members have, they can expect to run up against resistances caused by one or more of the following:

- doubts about people's motivation and competence;
- fear that people who think they have control will lose it;
- lack of confidence in leaders about their own competency;
- the perception that giving people influence will mean more work for leaders;
- the notion that to give people more influence will cost everybody more time; and
- the general fear of uncertainty and instability.

All these resistances have two things in common. First, they reflect fear of the unknown. Second, they reflect doubt about personal payoff. Every time I start a team development process with work units, people ask the same kinds of questions:

- "What will I be expected to do? Will I be expected to do something that I don't know how to do?"
- "What is the payoff? Am I going to be rewarded if I become more influential and help others become more influential?"

The only way to develop a team is through teamwork. All work units that develop themselves into fully functioning teams go through a "proof of concept phase." They grow into teams as they begin to function as teams. Being influential and extending influence are essential attributes of a team and are precisely what work units begin to do more and more of as they develop themselves into teams.

The only way to dispel the various myths associated with the process of influencing and the only way to overcome the resistances that members of work units have about increasing the opportunities for influence is for work units to manage the matter of influence themselves. This point is perhaps best illustrated with a few brief examples.

When work units participate in my seminars on team development, one of the exercises that they go through is to use the Competencies and Influence Grid (figure 4–2) to figure out for themselves how to target new opportunities for their members to be more influential. Two levels of activity are happening in the exercise. At the first level, the team is planning how to help members be more influential. At the second level, the work unit is practicing being influential by the very act of planning an action together. In other words, *the team is increasing the influence of its members in the very act of thinking about opportunities for increased influence.*

The first strategic consideration for teams to keep in mind about extending the influence of members is to recognize that they may find a number of resistances to overcome. The best way for teams to respond to these resistances is simply to make improving a team project.

A second strategic consideration related to improving the process of influencing is that it should always be clearly coupled with improving performance.

Coupling Influence with Improvement

Improving the process of influencing has an intensely practical purpose: to ensure that the team continues to perform at its highest level of potential. This means, of course, that the team must always be on a positive improvement slope.

Who knows most about the task being performed? Obviously, it is the person who has experience in performing it. Who is most likely to have the best information about how to improve the performance of a task? Obviously, it is the person who performs it. Who is most like to have the best information about work-flow processes? Obviously, it is the people who use it day in and day out. Who is most likely to be able to improve a work process? Obviously, it is the people who use it.

This litany of questions and answers can be extended to every aspect of a team's or organization's performance. Stimulating and encouraging people to be influential (let us never forget) is simply the practical way to make the fullest use of the competencies that team members have.

The standard against which every initiative for extending influence should be measured is quality. Every team member should be expected to take whatever action is necessary to improve the quality of ideas, of decisions, of problem solving, of work processes, and of production itself. Extending influence means that people are expected to stop an assembly line when errors or defects are discovered. It means that no change in a job task or work process is made unless the change has been tested and passed by the people it impacts.

When teams focus on the Informal Process of influencing, they should keep their goal clearly before them. The goal is not democracy or equality. The goal is always continuous improvement.

Each of us, in whatever job we have, should keep before us one fact: There is an international competitor out there that has one-half of our population, that has a land mass about the size of Montana, that has no significant amounts of oil, timber, coal, iron ore, fiber, or uranium. Japan is, of course, that competitor's name.

Japan has only one significant resource in any significant quantity, and that is its people. Japan has found ways to give people influence and thereby make the most of their competencies. Americans must find our own way.

If teams and organizations lose sight of just why they want people to have influence, they will turn this powerful tool for improvement into a game, a farce. When I work with teams and organizations that lack the hard-headed sense to recognize that influence means improvement, I hear statements like these:

- "I always give my people a chance to comment on what I'm planning to do. It makes them feel like they have a say even when I have already made up my mind."

- "I get paid to make decisions. I'm the one who's held responsible. I don't mind getting input from people, but when I know what's best, then that's what we are going to do."

- "People in this unit can have as much influence as they want. The fact is that they don't want it. I'm their supervisor, and they expect me to tell them what to do."

- "Each of us has a job to do. We are all good at our jobs. If we started checking with each other about what we planned to do, nothing would ever get done around here."

I have now touched on two strategic considerations relative to the Informal Process of influencing and improving. The third is that the process should be considered a way of life and not a program.

Influence and Improvement as a Way of Life

There are now many formal influence and involvement techniques, such as quality circles, suggestion systems, management boards, crew meetings, company hotlines, and various kinds of focused or special-purpose teams. Many companies are now deeply involved in TQM programs, which stress the need for employee involvement and influence.

Such formal programs are probably necessary just to get people's attention and to help organizations target the use of their resources. We should always keep in mind, however, that formal programs have serious limitations.

The trouble with programs is that they are programs. Just the idea of a program carries a lot of negative baggage. Often people view programs as they view the latest automobile sale: few people take seriously the overstated claims. No one truly believes that "this is the sale of the century," or that "this is the lowest price anywhere," or "name your own price because every car must go."

Like car sales, special programs in organizations have a credibility problem. Programs also tend to focus people on short-term goals and payoffs. It becomes easy to abandon programs when the payoffs are not forthcoming.

The Informal Process of influencing and improving must become a way of life for teams and organizations to benefit fully from it. The opportunity for mutual influence must become the norm for every conversation and interaction among team members. When teams are told to introduce some new work procedure, the automatic response must be that the whole team plans for the change. When new members are being considered for a team, team members should routinely be involved in the decision.

We need to move away from the notion that we must provide special opportunities for team members to be influential like placing them on a project team or a quality circle. Superior-work-team development and performance depends directly upon the team making continuous, day-to-day use of the special resource that each team member represents.

There are at least three special or strategic considerations that teams should keep in mind as they try to improve their process of influencing and improving.

- There can be strong resistances to extending influence.

- Influence should always be coupled clearly with improvement.

- Influencing and improving should be considered a way of life and not a program.

The final Informal Process in the model is **appreciating and celebrating.**

Appreciating and Celebrating

Members of superior work teams are unquestionably aware of their own value, and they are quite clear about the contributions that they make to the team's success. This clear sense of personal value is the result of a highly visible and dynamic Informal Process of appreciating and celebrating (Kinlaw 1989).

Appreciating and celebrating are expressed through two channels, one formal and the other informal. Both channels must be fully used because appreciating and celebrating are tied directly to a team's development and performance. Formal awards, such as promotions, bonuses, and citations, are needed. Formal awards, however, have a number of limitations, and they cannot by themselves communicate to team members their full value.

One limitation of formal awards is that their impact is often diluted because they are not timely enough. By the time they are received, the events that they commemorate may have long since passed. People have often said to me that their award didn't mean much because by the time they received the award, they had moved on to another job or the population of their work unit had changed. Awards clearly lose a lot of their impact when they are received among strangers.

A second limitation of formal awards is that they may not really communicate appreciation. In a number of organizations that have "employee of the month" programs, many employees do not feel it an honor to be the employee of the month. They feel that the reward is "passed around," or they feel that managers are told to identify a candidate at the last minute.

Aboard some U.S. Navy ships, one of the worst things that can happen to a crew member is to be made "sailor of the month." The fear is that other sailors will the view the recipient as a flunky.

A West Coast company gives an engineering achievement award to the individual who has made the most significant contribution to the success of some engineering project delivered to a customer. The problem is that the person singled out for the award always feels very self-conscious because he or she feels it inappropriate to accept an award that really should go to all the people who worked on the project.

A final limitation of formal awards is that these systems are rarely fully utilized, especially in large organizations.

One reason for this lack of use is that leaders who are required to initiate action for awards often do not know about all the awards that are available. Another is that formal awards usually require a good bit of paper work, and supervisors and other leaders may choose to avoid what they consider "extra" work.

Informal awards are likely to have more impact on people than formal ones. When I ask jobholders to tell me about something that happened to them that made them feel especially appreciated and valued by their organizations, better than 85 percent of the time they identify some informal action or event.

Here is an example. A woman in a seminar of mine described the following experience.

> I was a secretary at the time and had gone out of my way to help a group of mechanics who were responsible for the four tie-down posts that keep the Shuttle stable on the pad until the moment the engines are turned on.
>
> One afternoon, I received a telephone call from the shop

where these mechanics worked and was told that there was an emergency and would I please come down. I dropped everything and rushed down to the shop.

When I walked in the door, the mechanics were lined up with their large torque wrenches held up making an archway like the ones you see at military weddings. Only, of course, they use swords. I walked through the arch of wrenches to the end of the shop. They had set a table with a beautiful cake and had gotten a little combo (from who knows where) that was playing music. When I got through the arch, the music stopped and all the mechanics gathered around. Then one of them stepped forward and presented me with a sash (like the ones you see in a beauty contest). The sash read "Ms. Tie-Down Post of 1985." I can tell you that it was an experience that probably means more to me than anything that has ever happened to me at work.

A recent participant in my residential manager-education program gave me the following story of another creative informal award.

Our software manager has a thing for penguins. He has pictures of penguins of every kind posted all over his office. In one of our meetings, we got on the crazy idea of penguins wearing those surfing trunks called "jams." Later on, while I was walking through a store, I saw a stuffed doll of Opus, the penguin in the cartoon. The doll had on a beach hat and sandals.

As I looked at the doll, the idea popped into my mind to create an award for the software folks and pass it around each month to the top programmer. I named it on the spot the "Penguin Jam" award and bought the doll and a pair of jams for it. The way we finally set it up was that the person who got the award had to add something personal to it each time. If you can believe it, the "Penguin Jam" is one that people on my team really prize. It has become a real tradition.

Appreciating and celebrating is an Informal Process that is obvious in superior work teams. As teams go about strengthening the process, there are a few considerations that they should keep in mind.

Strategic Considerations for Strengthening Appreciation and Celebration

The following strategic considerations can serve as useful guidelines for strengthening appreciation and celebrating

- **There is more to appreciate and celebrate than superior performance.**
- **You can't do too much.**
- **Focus on the team.**

There Is More to Appreciate and Celebrate than Performance

One great advantage of informal acts of appreciation is that they can do more than just acknowledge superior performance. They can acknowledge people who show up day after day and do routine jobs that are not spectacular or even visible. They can tell people how courageous they are just for showing up. They can communicate special thanks when people patiently put up with bureaucratic delay and hostile customers and insensitive leaders.

Nobody shows much interest in tap water until it stops running. People usually take little interest in the grass around their buildings until they see that it hasn't been cut. As long as the people in accounting and payroll deliver the checks on time, they are rarely singled out for special praise.

When teams think about improving the Informal Process of appreciating and celebrating, they should consider a lot more than just performance. They should figure out how to become more sensitive to people who do the dirty or routine jobs. They should start celebrating the triumphs that people make when they patiently persevere in the face of bureaucratic delay and inertia.

You Can't Do Too Much

The various surveys that I have conducted over the past few years with organizations and work teams show that the three most serious problems are that jobholders believe that

- their organizations and teams do not have clear improvement goals and objectives;

- people have insufficient influence over their jobs, their work units, and their total organizations; and

- they are insufficiently appreciated and valued by their work units or organizations.

In all the seminars that I have conducted and in all the direct contacts that I have had with hundreds of work units, I have never run into people who felt that they had been thanked too often. Some people nonetheless have the odd notion that "you can thank people too much" or "you can overdo this business of appreciation."

I would like to challenge any team to overdo appreciating and celebrating the importance and value of its members. Having never seen such a phenomenon, I would very much like to observe it at first hand.

We know that too little appreciation impacts negatively on performance. We have not the slightest hint that too much appreciation has a negative impact on performance.

Focus on the Team

The Informal Process of appreciation and celebrating can be a very powerful tool for developing superior work teams. For it to be such, the team must focus on the team more than on individuals.

Individual awards and celebrations are important, but team success and performance must have the highest priority. In the organizations with which I have consulted over past ten years, there has been almost a ten-to-one ratio of individual to team awards. And this ratio reflects only what goes on in formal systems. I imagine that the ratio of individual to team awards would be even greater for informal awards.

Summary

In this chapter I have described in detail the Informal Processes of the model and discussed strategic considerations that should be taken into account when teams set out to improve their Informal Processes.

The four Informal Processes are:

- communicating and contacting
- responding and adapting
- influencing and improving, and
- appreciating and celebrating.

Strategic considerations should be taken into account when improving each of the Informal Processes. For communicating and contacting:

1. Never underestimate the difficulty in creating free, open, easy communication and contact in a team. Informal communication and contact are often not the norm in work units, and there may be considerable resistance to such a process.

2. The process of communicating and contacting can impact on a team's performance only when it is a quality process, when people have the requisite interpersonal communication skills.

For responding and adapting:

1. People have often developed habits and mindsets that resist the idea of responsiveness.

2. Creating high levels of responsiveness and adaptability requires that the process be reinforced over and over again.

For influencing and improving:

1. There can also be strong resistances to extending influence.

2. Influence should always be coupled clearly with improvement.

3. Influencing and improving should be considered as a way of life and not as a program.

For appreciating and celebrating:

1. Don't forget that there is more to celebrate than superior performance.

2. Don't be afraid of doing too much.

3. Focus on the team.

The payoffs from the four Informal Processes that I have identified in the Model for Superior Development and Performance can be extensive. An improvement in any one of them will create improvements in the others. And improvement in the processes will strengthen every other element and subelement in the model.

I have now discussed two of the four primary elements in the Model for Superior Team Development and Performance: Results and Informal Processes. In the next chapter I will discuss the third element in the model, Feelings.

6

Focusing on Team Feelings

In the two previous chapters I have discussed two of the primary elements in the Model for Superior Team Development and Performance: Results and Informal Processes. In this chapter, I will discuss Feelings, the third primary element in the model.

Members of superior work teams consistently describe a different set of feelings from those of members from poorly developed teams. These Feelings are as persistent as they are pervasive.

Members of superior work teams do experience at times the negative feelings that members of other work units have. They feel put upon, frustrated, and angry, or they feel unhappy, anxious, and despondent.

What is distinctive about superior work teams, however, is that these negative feelings do not persist. They find resolution and are generally overpowered by positive feelings.

Members of superior work teams talk about their feelings in a language that is both energetic and colorful. A member of a lagging crew puts it this way:

> People used to ask me how the hell I could enjoy such dirty work. I guess I never thought of it as dirty. I sure never felt sorry for myself. How the hell could I? There wasn't a guy in my crew that ever ducked a tough job or sat on their butts letting somebody else do the work. We were really tight. I can't say that I liked all of the other guys. There were some I wouldn't want to take home or anything like that. But I've never worked with a better crew before or since.

A sales representative describes his feelings as follows:

You couldn't help but feel that you were part of a team. We were so focused on outselling our competitors that we didn't have time to fight with each other. We even had a sign in our conference room that read "The enemy is not your buddy, it's the competition."

Analysis of the way superior-work-team members describe their experiences shows that at least five kinds of feelings are typical of them:

- inclusion
- commitment
- loyalty
- pride,
- trust

Inclusion

The words and phrases that people use in my seminars and interviews suggest just how central the experience of **inclusion** is.

- "sense of belonging"
- "We were all good friends"
- "closeness"
- "accepted"
- "I felt I was important"
- "I knew what was going on"
- "People took me seriously"
- "respected"
- "We took credit for our work as a team"

In superior work teams there are no first-, second-, or third-class citizens. Actions or conditions create a sense of inclusion.

- Team members get the information that affects their job and their life in the organization.

- The right team members attend the right meetings.

- Team members have a say when decisions are made that affect them.

- New ideas are encouraged and treated with respect.

- Team members have a fair chance at challenging work.

- High levels of appreciation are expressed to team members for their value to the team.

- Team members receive quick response from other team members when they ask for help.

- Team members demonstrate a practical concern for each other's well-being.

- Team members have a chance to demonstrate their full competence.

- Team members all participate in a variety of social activities.

Symbols are powerful tools to either create or subvert inclusion. A contractor friend told me the following story.

> I have had a number of the same clients for many, many years. The managers in one of my client organizations have told me on a number of occasions that they considered me as part of the team because I was a person who was trusted by everyone and that people knew that I would never betray a confidence. Sometimes when I get a new contract or purchase order I have a little trouble believing that I am really part of the team, however, because the first word that jumps out at me is *vendor*. I always somehow picture a vendor as a guy standing on a street corner turning an organ grinder with a monkey on his shoulder with a tin cup begging for handouts.

Richardo Semler, president of Semco, maintains that one of the biggest enemies of performance is managers who are jealous of their power and prerogatives (Semler 1989). But the problem of prerogatives exists not only among managers but in the whole work force. Prerogatives of any kind—no matter who benefits from them—must have a clearly functional reason for existing to serve the purposes of team development. When anyone gets special treatment on a team, the reason for the treatment must be clearly connected to the person's performance and value to the team. For example, aboard ship, the oncoming watch goes to the head of the chow line for reasons that are obvious to everyone: The oncoming watch must be fed in order to relieve the section that is currently on watch.

Most privileges, however, have no such obviously functional value. The practice of reserved parking, for example, has very little to commend it. The message is that the people who have reserved parking places are more important than those who don't. Every single day that a worker hunts around to find a place to park and must drive past empty spaces reserved for managers, supervisors, and staff personnel, that worker gets a clear lesson in relative importance.

One fascinatingly misguided practice of some companies is that they select an "employee of the month," based on that person's work, then give the winner a reserved parking place for one month. The message is that people must do something special to get a reserved spot for even a month, while members of the hierarchy get their spots without doing anything special to earn them.

A short time ago, I listened with disbelief to two senior managers discussing their concern about engineers who "don't act like engineers. They don't seem to be conscious that they are professionals. When you see them on the floor, you can't tell them from the technicians."

As I listened I thought of a movie, a comedy, in which one of the funniest scenes was when one worker is indoctrinating a new worker into the culture of the organization. The new worker is told that in that organization the most important thing to keep in mind is the distinction between the "suits" and the "nonsuits." The rule is that nonsuits (the workers) never under any circumstances speak to the suits (management) unless the suits speak first.

Team members must feel a strong sense of inclusion if a team is to continue to develop and reach sustained levels of superior performance. Inclusion is created and maintained by both functional and symbolic aspects of a team's environment. Teams must ensure that people are treated with respect and that they have a chance to demonstrate their competence. Teams must also be sensitive to the symbols that suggest inclusion and those that reinforce the sense of hierarchy and degrees of importance and value.

Commitment

People on superior teams describe themselves as

- being focused
- looking forward to going to work
- caring about results and how well the team did
- taking it quite personally when the team did not meet its goals
- making personal sacrifices to make sure the team succeeded
- being determined to succeed
- being single-minded, and
- never giving up.

In *Coaching for Commitment* (Kinlaw 1989) I suggested that two indicators can help determine just how **committed** people are. One is the degree to which people are focused on a goal, and the other is the degree of sacrifice that people are willing to make to reach the goal. These two indicators show a high level of commitment among people who describe their experiences on superior work teams.

The lead mechanic in an air compressor team gives this colorful description of his present experience in his shop.

> When you show up for work in our shop, you'd better have your pants hitched up and your shoes laced. We mean business and that's no . . . When our shop got organized, the whole . . . operation was in a whole lot of hurt. Within one year, we achieved a rate of zero downtime for air supply to every building, and we haven't had a single tool fail in any shop because it didn't have air.

While other work units struggle to maintain barely satisfactory levels of performance through control, superior work teams achieve superior levels of performance through commitment. A commitment to quality on the part of every single person who touches a process, a product, or a service is the only proven way to ensure outputs that are 100 percent fit to use, 100 percent of the time. No organization has ever shown that that level of quality could be achieved by quality inspectors and engineers. There is simply no contest between teams that develop commitment in their members and those that depend on the grudging compliance of members to achieve results.

Loyalty

Commitment refers to the many different feelings that members of superior work teams have about their teams' goals, objectives, and priorities. The term *loyalty* captures the way members describe their feelings toward each other. Some typical expressions are:

- "I think we really cared what happened to each other."

- "We depended on each other so much, you just had to take care of your buddies. There was no other way you could get the job done."

- "We had such a reputation that we could get the very best people to work in our shop. We just started out with the best, and that's how we always thought of each other."

- "Nobody tried to show anybody else up. The old hands were really good about helping the new guys learn the ropes."

- "I think we all operated on the assumption that if anybody screwed up, it was everybody's fault. It just never seemed important to waste time finding a fall guy."

Just what happens to work units when loyalty among jobholders doesn't exist is demonstrated in an experience I had in working with a security unit at a government installation some years ago. I was contacted by management and presented with a set of their concerns and issues. Most of these were the typical sort of things like, "Our supervisors aren't acting like leaders," "Our employees aren't motivated," "Our people aren't sufficiently professional."

All these statements were too general to be treated as problems. And as is usually the case, none of these general statements even hinted at what the real problems turned out to be. The underlying problems that I finally identified were, first, that promotions and assignments were given out according to the whims and biases of the chief of security and other senior officers, and second, that guards were encouraged to "snitch" on their peers and to bring their stories and complaints directly to the senior officers without first discussing them with their peers.

This experience demonstrates forcefully just how interrelated the feelings characteristic of superior work teams are. Without loyalty in the unit, there was no commitment to a common set of performance goals. If there was any common goal among the rank and file, it was survival. Without loyalty and commitment, there was very little trust and very little for people to feel much pride about. And with all these negative feelings, members of the unit certainly did not feel any degree of inclusion.

In superior work teams loyalty becomes visible in at least two sets of behaviors. First, members go out of their way to ensure the success of their peers. Second, members give their colleagues the benefit of the doubt when they have apparently failed to meet an obligation or fulfill a commitment.

The way members of superior teams feel about the success of their fellow team members is captured in what a member of a print shop had to say about loyalty.

> I always had the feeling that my gang was truly interested in making sure we all got our jobs done. We used to joke a lot about our mistakes and mess-ups. We even had a "spilled ink" award that we presented to the person who had screwed up in some spectacular way. But underneath it all, we really cared about each other. On a day-to-day basis we all went out of our way to help each other look good and get the job done.

The importance of giving other team members the benefit of the doubt is illustrated by the story of a manager of a team that was responsible for a large computerized inventory control system.

Our team was responsible for keeping the system up and running. So many operations depended on the system that when we had a problem, it always showed up in a hurry, and it was very visible to everyone. Our team had to give a status report to our division chief every morning at 7:15 A.M. If there was ever an opportunity to "shoot the messenger" and find fault, that morning review session was really it. I mean, it was like being in charge of the electric lights or something. Nobody really notices as long as the lights are on. People just take it for granted. But look out if the lights go off. Then all hell breaks lose.

Well, it was like that with the inventory system. It worked from our mainframe, and our users were scattered all over our operating area. If the system or any part of it went down, our boss got instant feedback. At any rate, what I think has been so incredible is that our division chief has never treated us as though we set out to make the system fail. He has just always assumed that we are working our butts off to keep it going.

So when something happened and we had to tell him some bad news at our 7:15 session, he would always respond by asking us to tell him what we were doing about it and if we needed his help in any way.

Loyalty is a distinctive feeling among members of superior work teams. You see loyalty in action all the time on these teams. People go out of their way to ensure their colleagues' success, and they assume that when things do go wrong, their colleagues did not set out to make them go wrong.

Pride

A number of specific kinds of behaviors visible among the members of superior work teams give clear definition of what **pride** means.

- Members work hard at getting feedback, and they know how they and their teams are doing at all times.

- Feedback is taken seriously as a chance to improve and is not responded to defensively.

- Members believe that what they do is important and know how their products and services are tied to the organization's goals and final outputs.

- Members participate in setting performance goals and standards for themselves and for the whole team.

- Members have a strong orientation toward the future and fully expect to exceed their own current levels of performance.

- There is a much greater emphasis on team achievement and success than on individual achievement and success.

Some of the specific words and phrases that I have recorded from superior-work-team members are these:

- "I felt responsible. Everything about the job that went right or wrong reflected directly on me."

- "I felt confident. I felt as if I could handle just about anything that I was asked to do."

- "We all felt as if we really counted, as if we were worth something. We just had that feeling that the whole company knew that when people came to us, they were going to get a job done that was the best."

- "We had saved so many people's bacon so often that we had an unlimited number of chits that we could call in at any time. We could get things done faster and better than anybody else because we had developed our own private support system."

Work and self-worth are the two factors in pride that interact with each other and that tend to increase the strong sense of pride found in superior work teams. When people do something of obvious worth, they feel a strong sense of personal worth. It is a strong sense of personal worth that leads people to want to express that worth in what they do.

Superior work teams fuel this interaction between performance and personal worth. On superior work teams, people have the opportunity to feel worth not only because of what they do as individuals, but because they are valued members of a whole team that is performing well. A member of a section in a comptroller's office put it this way:

> I actually felt important the day I was hired into the section—even before I had done anything. The whole company knew that this section could get just about anybody it wanted. There was a waiting list for any opening that might occur. And later on, when I actually began to make a contribution, I felt as if I were one of the luckiest people in the company. The people in the section recognized that I was doing really good work, and the whole team was recognized as something very special in the company.

Trust

In superior work teams, **trust** has some very specific meanings. It means that members

- do what they say they are going to do;
- are sometimes painfully straightforward and never conceal information from each other that they feel their colleagues should have;
- can be depended on because they are viewed by their colleagues as having the knowledge and skills to perform;
- are willing to listen to each other and to defer to each other because they expect reliable information and good ideas from each other.

Other kinds of behaviors work against developing trust on work teams.

- People are checked up on frequently and are required to give status reports often about how they are doing or how the job is coming along.

- People feel as if they are being micromanaged, that decisions are made that they should make, and that they are given detailed direction on how to do their jobs.

- There is a general lack of communication. People are often surprised by plans, changes, and problems that they should have known about in advance.

- There is a lot of secrecy about pay, promotions, awards, and job assignments.

Trust, of course, interacts with the other key feelings of inclusion, commitment, loyalty, and pride. All of these feelings feed on each other. It is easy to feel included in a group of people whom one trusts. It is easy to become committed to the goals and values of an organization when we trust the people who communicate these goals and values.

Here are a couple of examples of what trust feels like in superior work teams. A secretary describes her relationship with her network team of company secretaries this way.

I was a secretary in the company for a good many years before the secretaries started thinking of themselves as a team. We rarely saw each other because we all worked in different parts of the company. We all did a lot of business by phone, but we largely thought of ourselves as members of teams made up of our boss and the other staff members.

A couple of years ago we started taking a proactive position about ourselves, and one of the first things that we did was to request some of the same kind of training that we saw managers and supervisors going to. We were especially interested in a total quality management seminar that the company was offering to work teams.

We weren't a work team but we were able to get a special seminar put together on total quality management for just the secretaries. It turned out to be a tremendous team-development experience. Ever since the seminar we have been meeting regularly and I can tell you that there is all the difference in the world in the way we work together.

What's really different is that we have developed a lot of trust among ourselves. We have begun to appreciate all the kinds of help that we can give to each other. We go out of our way to keep each other informed about everything that goes on. We get help from each other whenever we need it.

We have surprised everybody, especially our bosses, with the way we can get information and solve problems that no one else can manage. And the secret is simply that we now think of ourselves as a team, and we know that we can trust each other to help when we need it.

These, then, are the five key feelings that are typical of superior work teams and superior teamwork. This list is certainly not exhaustive but these particular feelings are so pervasive and predictable that they can be used as baselines to assess team development and as targets for improving team development.

In the next section of this chapter, I will discuss some strategic considerations that teams should keep in mind as they consider strengthening these Feelings among their members.

Strategic Considerations for Developing Superior Work-Team Feelings

Because all of the five Feelings associated with superior work teams are so closely related and interactive, it is all but impossible to influence one without influencing one or more of the others. The following strategic considerations, therefore, may be considered as applying to each of the feelings independently as well as to all of them taken as a whole.

When teams consider what might be done to strengthen the Feelings discussed in this chapter, there are at least two strategic considerations that they should keep before them.

First, feelings cannot be built directly. Feelings result as indirect consequences of persistent conditions that exist in a team's environment. Second, the most persistent and impactful aspect of a team's environment is its values.

Feelings Are Indirect Consequences

The five Feelings that are identified in the Model for Superior Team Development and Performance are very much like key indicators for good health. If inclusion, commitment, loyalty, pride, and trust are strong, the team is strong and healthy.

Everything that goes on in a team affects the feelings of its members, and the feelings of its members interact with all the other key elements in the Model for Superior Team Development and Performance to determine the total performance of the team.

It is absurd to imagine that team members can be directed to feel inclusion, or commitment, or loyalty, or anything else. These feelings result when the team persistently

- clarifies its purposes, values, work processes, and individual responsibilities;

- shows appreciation to its members (individually and collectively) for their value to the team;

- ensures that everyone has the knowledge and skills to perform up to the very highest standards; and

- extends opportunities for members to have influence over their jobs, the team, and the larger organization (Kinlaw 1989).

The operational word in strengthening the key Feelings is *persistence*. The key Feelings are not engendered and maintained by slogans or quick fixes. They are created by clarifying and reclarifying the team's purposes, priorities, values, and responsibilities through every decision that is made and every action that is taken. The major barrier to strengthening the key Feelings is inconsistency.

Imagine a team member who is told to produce a quality report, then is told to do it within absurd time limits.

Or imagine a team that talks about itself as intending to satisfy its customers 100 percent of the time, then does not establish an ongoing feedback mechanism for maintaining the most intimate kind of contact with its customers.

I know of an engineering support firm that is in the process of decline and possible demise because it announced that its intention was to provide its customers with quality designs and drawings, but it communicates daily to its drafters and engineers (by its emphasis on meeting schedules) that its real goal is to get as much work out the door as possible, then worry about fixing it later. People don't produce very well for very long when they work in environments with conflicting values.

The point that I am making is a simple and obvious one. Values must be communicated and reinforced through consistent action and decision making. One organization uses the phrase "walk as you talk" to underscore the importance of everyone in the company making its publicized values fully congruent with its actions.

Many organizations and teams claim that their most valuable resource is their people. But this fairly popular claim is a bit difficult to take seriously when

- training is offered grudgingly and supervisors nominate people for training not on the basis of need but on the basis of "who can be spared";

- training is offered only on employee time, such as Saturdays and after work hours;

- people are herded together in spaces that are more appropriate for sheltering cattle than for serious mental activity;

- people are treated like children, and every minute of their work-day is regulated and supervised;

- the formal and informal systems for communicating appreciation to people are inadequate;

- supervisors are rarely evaluated on their performance in developing the knowledge and skills of their people; and

- management often awards special privileges and special benefits to itself (without, I might say, giving jobholders a vote).

Teams should keep in mind as they consider strengthening the five key Feelings that these feelings are an indirect result of a multitude of consistent decisions and actions. Slogans and "motivational" talks will not build inclusion, or commitment, or loyalty. Professions of quality, openness, or risk taking will not build pride or trust. The key Feelings that characterize superior teams are built by the whole team "walking like it talks."

People in superior teams feel a special way because they work in special environments. To grow into superior work teams, every work unit must have an obvious set of values that provides the bedrock for every day-by-day decision and action.

Values Are the Major Leverage Point

A second strategic consideration is to recognize that building a clear set of values is the best leverage point teams have for strengthening the key Feelings.

I have already touched on the importance of values in discussing the need for consistency in decisions and actions. Consistency and values are closely related. Consistency cannot be established through rules, except in some kind of totally routinized production or work process. In the majority of jobs there are too many unexpected events and problems for each one to be covered by a rule.

Superior work teams recognize that consistently high performance can be built not on rules but only on values. In fact, it is a striking aspect of superior work teams that they have so few rules.

Once a team has established the value, for example, that it intends to have "enthusiastically positive customers," or that it will "do everything right the first time," or that "every worker will be treated with respect," then the day-to-day decisions of people are simple.

In a segment of the old Ma Bell network where I consulted some years ago, everything that each jobholder did was focused on the same goal. If you asked any lineman, secretary, crew member, or manager the question, "What is your top priority?" you would get the same answer: "Dial tone." Members of that company knew what took precedence over everything else.

When training offices in organizations ask me to conduct seminars and workshops, I used to ask them questions like, "Have you conducted a needs assessment?" "What is the problem that you are trying to fix?" "When was the last time you conducted the kind of training in which you are now interested?" I discovered over the years that organizations often go about trying to change values through training *before the values have been communicated or established as a company norm.*

My strategy now is much simpler. I just ask the training offices what company values they think my training will support. It is absurd to imagine that any kind of training is going to be effective if it is occurring in an environment whose values are not fully congruent with the training.

It is pretty easy to tell when training is not congruent with the values of the company's environment. When this happens, the trainer starts getting questions like

- "Has my supervisor been to this program?"
- "Does upper management really support this stuff?"
- "Do our bosses know what this program is all about?"

The key Feelings can be established, nurtured, and strengthened only by undeviatingly consistent support of a core set of values. Policies and practices, rules and regulations don't build superior teams—they only build conformity.

The values that teams develop should give every team member a clear answer to questions like

- "What do we intend about customer satisfaction?"

- "How do we expect team members to interact and communicate?"

- "What are our standards for our services and products?"

- "What do we intend about continuous improvement?"

- "What do we expect from each other?"

Summary

Five key Feelings make up the third key element in the Model for Superior Team Development and Performance. Two strategic considerations can help guide teams as they undertake to strengthen these Feelings.

The key Feelings are

- inclusion
- commitment
- loyalty
- pride, and
- trust.

The two strategic considerations are

1. Feelings cannot be built directly. Feelings result from the persistent conditions that exist in a team's environment.

2. The most persistent and impactful aspect of a team's environment is its values.

I have now covered three of the primary elements in the Model for Superior Team Development and Performance: Results, Informal Processes, and Feelings. In the next chapter I will discuss the fourth primary element, Leadership.

7
Focusing on Team Leadership

I have now covered three of the primary elements in the Model for Superior Team Development and Performance: Results, Informal Processes, and Feelings. The final primary element in the model is Leadership.

Leadership, as the term is used in the model, carries one specific meaning: It means leadership of teams.

An enormous amount of information is available on leadership and leadership theories. One of the best reviews and compilations of the literature can be found in *Stogdills's Handbook of Leadership* (Stogdill 1981). A surprising aspect of the literature on leadership, however, is that little attention has been given to the leadership of work teams.

There are political and military theories of leadership. There are theories that focus on the psychological traits of leaders. There are theories that describe leadership in terms of human relationships and interaction. There are theories that describe managerial and executive leadership. There are a few theories on work group leadership (Hackman and Walton 1986). I have found no theories, however, that adequately address the subject of the leadership of superior work teams that do real work and that are held responsible for their performance.

It will be some time before an adequate theory of leadership of superior work teams is produced. The interest in this field is only beginning to develop; you will certainly not find such a theory in this chapter. What you will find is a description of Leadership as it exists in the superior work teams that I have observed or that have been described to me.

The purposes of this chapter are

- to discuss the special characteristics of the Leadership of superior work teams; and

- to describe the special Leadership roles that exist in superior teams.

The discussion of work team Leadership that follows is based on my experience with teams that are organized with a supervisor or lead and a number of team members. I do believe, however, that what I have learned about leadership in traditionally organized work teams can be applied to teams organized more innovatively, like self-directed or self-managing teams.

Leadership in a superior work team is a set of roles and functions. These roles can be occupied by a single person or by the team as a whole. These functions can be performed by one person or by many persons. If Leadership is understood as a set of roles and functions, what I have to say in the following pages can be applied to both traditional and nontraditional work teams.

Special Characteristics of
Superior-Work-Team Leadership

Leadership in superior work teams is radically different from the way leadership is traditionally understood. In its most general terms, leadership is described as the process of gaining followers. The logic is that to be a leader, one must have followers. Leadership requires "followership." This kind of logic immediately presents problems for understanding leadership in superior work teams. Leadership in superior work teams does not mean creating followers. It means being a team player and creating team players.

Some of the characteristics that make Leadership in superior teams distinctive are:

- It means **leading through teamwork.**

- It means **staying focused both on team development and on team performance.**

Primary Orientation toward the Team and Teamwork

Team leaders are first, last, and always team players. They approach every task and decision as a potential opportunity for teamwork. Their fundamental orientation toward teamwork has some fairly dramatic implications for the way team leaders think and act. It means that team leaders focus

- on team performance more than on individual performance; and

- on commitment as the way to achieve superior performance, not on control.

Team versus Individual Performance. Team leaders are focused on the team and on encouraging maximum team performance more than they are focused on individuals and how to maximize individual performance. In the same way, they view performance problems as team problems rather than individual problems.

Focusing on the team represents a radical departure from conventional wisdom. Just how radical this departure is can be seen by looking at the content of most manager, supervisor, and leadership education programs.

The way organizations go about educating their supervisors and managers provides a good indication of just how most people view leadership in organizations. Most education programs have a clear bias toward managing individuals.

Manager and supervisor education programs typically cover topics like

- motivating employees
- delegating
- managing performance
- employee development, and
- performance appraisal.

Every one of these topics reinforces the notion that the leader's job is to get the most out of individuals. The assumption is that if each individual works harder, the total performance of the group will improve. So education programs teach leaders

- how to strengthen the motivation to work of individual employees by using Maslow's hierarchy, Herzberg's job enrichment, behavior modification, or some form of expectancy theory;

- how to increase the output of individual employees by delegating more responsibility to each employee;

- how to improve individual performance by giving clear direction, feedback, and rewards;

- how to develop individuals through career planning and individual training plans; and

- how to manage total individual performance through performance planning and performance appraisals.

In a current favorite session in most leadership-education programs, supervisors and managers analyze their styles and practices. These sessions use a variety of questionnaires and feedback instruments to assess and rate the practices and styles of the individual manager or supervisor. All these questionnaires and instruments, in one way or another, actually assess how the individual leader interacts with other individuals. Again, the bias toward individual behavior and of leading individuals is apparent.

Leaders of superior work teams do not make less of individuals and individual performance than do traditional leaders. Superior-work-team leaders, in fact, have higher expectations for individual performance than do leaders who focus on individuals. Superior leaders know that individual performance and development are maximized through teamwork. They know that the best way to manage individual performance problems is through the power of team membership and team norms.

Other work-unit leaders waste a lot of time managing performance problems that need never have occurred or that could have been handled by the team.

In well-developed teams with well-developed values and norms, many of the problems that worry other leaders just don't arise. As

I have discussed in chapter 6, core values and clear norms are characteristic of superior work teams. When norms about timeliness, cooperation, reliability, integrity, and the like are clear, many of the traditional performance problems just don't occur. Members of well-developed teams will typically do everything they can to not break a norm. They value too highly being a member of the team. Breaking a norm calls their own membership into question.

Performance problems in superior work teams are handled by the team. Everybody enforces and reinforces the values and norms. A member of an engineering branch puts it this way.

> The worst feeling I ever had on my team was the time I felt I had let my buddies down. There was a design review meeting that we had with a customer, and I had the lead. There was this real obnoxious character at the meeting who had not attended any of the earlier review meetings and who hadn't bothered to read himself into the project. He kept raising irrelevant questions and pontificating about really stupid issues, and I finally lost my cool and let him know what I thought of his contributions. I think I pretty well let him know that he had flawed genes and was playing with a partial deck.
>
> Well, my whole team was put on report, and we got in deep yogurt with the customer and also with our division chief. The tough part for me was that the rest of the team let me know that I had thrown months of their hard work out the window. I didn't mind what the chief said to me, but I minded like hell what my team said to me.

A member of an expendable rocket-launch team told me how his supervisor went about establishing some very important team norms.

> When John became our supervisor, he made an instant impression. The first day he came on board, he called us all together and made a speech. He said that his primary function was to get everything that he could for us. He was going to spend his time getting us the training that we wanted and all awards and promotions that we deserved. He said that he was going to spend his time doing everything that he could to provide us with the best possible work environment. He then said that if he was going to

spend his time doing all those things, we would have to do the work and solve most of the problems.

John kept his word. And I can tell you this—he was the best supervisor I ever had, and we had the best team that I can remember working on.

Because the leaders of superior work teams focus on teamwork and team performance, they naturally focus on team rewards more than on individual awards. In traditional work groups and organizations, there are many more individual awards than team awards. Their emphasis is on individual performance, individual entrepreneurship, and individual competition. But in teams whose leaders are focused on team performance, you will find team awards for quality, productivity, cost savings, innovative ideas, perfect attendance, continuous improvement, cost avoidance, and customer satisfaction.

Once teams develop the kind of intense team consciousness that I have found in superior work teams team members themselves begin to consider all their awards to be team awards. In a shop in a Florida engineering firm, a mechanic received a $15,000 award for suggesting that two large air compressors that were slated for salvage be repaired, and for putting the compressors to use in a large heating plant that the company was running. Rather than taking the reward himself, the mechanic directed that it be split among all his team members.

Commitment versus Control. When leaders focus on the team and teamwork, they naturally depart from the traditional management and supervisory model of control to a model of managing by commitment. As we have seen in chapter 5, one outcome of extending influence is to create a stronger level of commitment among team members to the team's total performance. And in chapter 6, we have seen that commitment is one of the five key Feelings that typify superior teams. Commitment was contrasted with control as the only strategy for achieving sustained superior performance.

Building employee commitment—not building controls—is characteristic of the leaders of superior work teams. These leaders know intuitively or from their experience that controls can produce (at the most) only satisfactory performance. The control model is limited for several reasons (Kinlaw 1989).

First, it has always been a challenge for leaders of work groups to get people to do what they want them to do. People have private goals and priorities that are not fully congruent (all or part of the time) with leaders' or organizations' goals and priorities. And people want to demonstrate their own competence by doing things "their own way." Being independent is a value too deeply rooted in our American culture to be fully managed, no matter what kind of controls we institute. It is not by accident that Frank Sinatra periodically croons live and on recordings, "I did it my way."

A number of studies are telling us (as if our own real-life experiences were not enough) that we can expect people's demands for job autonomy to increase further. Recent studies such as those conducted by the Public Agenda Foundation (Yankelovich and Immerwahr 1983) tell us that American workers have always valued good pay, a safe and convenient workplace, and good fringe benefits. But jobholders of the baby-boom generation have brought a new set of psychological demands to their jobs. People are looking for more from their jobs. They want work that is interesting and challenging. And they want more control or autonomy in their jobs.

A second reason the control model of managing does not work very well is that more and more people have more and more discretionary time and energy that they can choose to give or not to give to their jobs. This has come about partly because of the kinds of jobs that people now do. We have seen an enormous shift in jobs away from routinized jobs in the industrial and manufacturing sector and toward the service and professional sector.

I have tested this idea of discretionary effort with thousands of jobholders—from gate guards and refractories mechanics to aerospace engineers and scientists. My findings are consistent. Most people indicate that they could give 15 percent to 20 percent more or less effort in their jobs *and nobody would know the difference—especially their supervisors.*

A third limitation to the traditional control model is that most people know more about their specific jobs than anyone else, including their supervisors.

There are several reasons for this. One is that people typically work in jobs that are so complex that they require a great deal of specialization. Also, the technologies of these jobs is always changing.

A personal example illustrates my point. My own small business depends upon its computer capability to survive. When I first started using a certain word-processing software, the user's manual was about an inch thick. The last time I upgraded, the user's manual was about five inches thick. I could literally devote all my time to fully mastering that software. It is easy to understand why people are able to make a living just teaching others how to use one or two software applications.

Most managers will usually admit that their secretaries know more about their business than they themselves do. Now, the gap between what secretaries and managers know is becoming even wider. Consider the armamentarium of most secretaries. They have PCs and modems. They manage and use networks, electronic mail, corporate calendars, fax machines, and databases. The changes in the knowledge bases of secretaries is certain to increase the dependence of managers and the autonomy of secretaries.

A fourth limitation to the control model is that work environments are often so filled with problems and are so unstable—if not chaotic—that leaders cannot predict what needs to be done in order to achieve the results that they are after. One important value that jobholders have for their companies is that they solve problems, they take care of the unexpected, and they take advantage of unanticipated opportunities. People are often most valuable because they do what no one could have predicted beforehand would need doing.

A fifth limitation to the control model is that controls not take full advantage of the human resources that are available in a work group. Leaders who operate from the control model consistently underutilize people and make poor use of their potential. The reason is that they fail to look for ways to extend people's influence and thereby give them more opportunities to demonstrate their competencies.

In this section I have discussed one of two characteristics that distinguish superior-work-team leadership from traditional leadership—its primary orientation in performing every aspect of work is toward the team and teamwork.

The second characteristic of superior-work-team leadership is that it is always focused on both team development and team performance.

Staying Focused on Both Team Development and Team Performance

Superior-work-team leaders recognize that team development and team performance are inseparable. They know that the more fully developed the team is, the better it will perform.

One of the most consistent and glaring errors that work-team leaders commit is that they stay so focused on getting the job done that they fail to build the team's potential for doing the job. Team development is the primary means for building the team's potential.

Over and over again, my experience with work-group leaders is they somehow imagine that the development of their work units into fully functioning teams will take place as a natural result of people being involved together in the same unit. The most common underlying cause of problems in work groups is that the group has never developed into a team.

Superior leaders understand

- that team development and team performance are part of the same inseparable process; and

- that work groups develop into teams only when they make a conscious decision to do so, then devote time and other resources to developing themselves into a team.

I recently conducted a survey of work groups in a design engineering group of some 350 people. Twenty-six work groups were involved, and the survey looked at team development and team performance. I followed up with a sample set of work groups to determine how the groups had used the survey data, what changes they had targeted, and exactly how they planned to reach their targets.

Here are a couple of my findings. First, the groups that scored high on the portions of the survey that measured team development have made better use of the survey to improve their performance than the groups that scored low on team development. Second, the groups that used teamwork to analyze their data have developed far more concrete initiatives to improve their performance than those groups in which the group's supervisor assumed responsibility for the data.

Teamwork is the key to both team development and superior performance. Superior team leaders understand that teams don't perform one minute, then develop themselves into teams the next.

The Model for Superior Team Development and Performance provides a number of ways to see just how clearly team development and team performance are associated. Take for example the key Results,

- maximum use of a team's human resources;
- superior outputs against all odds; and
- continuous improvement.

Only fully developed teams can attain these Results. I have observed over and over again just how critical is the connection between team development and team results. Here are a couple of examples that I have selected from a very large file.

One group had been in existence for about a year. People had been assigned to the group without consultation with the prospective supervisor. The group was given two older engineers who were near retirement, six recently graduated engineers, and a secretary who had very poor interpersonal skills and who had been previously on probation for poor performance. The group supervisor responded to one interpersonal and performance crisis after the other. Each time he went on leave, he returned to face one or more major catastrophes. Periodically, he was hauled on the mat by his boss and told to straighten his group out. He never made the connection between team development and performance, and so he never focused on ways to involve the team in solving its own problems—through teamwork. My last information indicated that the group had not improved and that senior management was considering ways to reorganize it out of existence.

Another example is a group that was described to me by a consultant. The group was in charge of a variety of training and personnel functions. The group's senior manager had been replaced, and the new manager decided to have a team-building retreat. He decided that because the team was made up largely of experienced human-resource professionals, it would not require a trained facilitator. His group of trained professionals acquiesced to his decision. But without a trained facilitator, the retreat degenerated into a very large brouhaha. No resolution of all the problems that were surfaced at the retreat has been attempted, and the many interpersonal issues have never been resolved. The group's performance has been acknowledged by most of its members as marginal, yet no one has made any serious attempt to connect the group's performance to its level of team development.

Superior-work-team leaders know that superior performance is possible only where there is superior-work-team development. These leaders know that they must focus on developing the team in order to achieve superior performance.

Superior Leadership Roles

At least three roles are associated with the leaders of superior work teams. These are

- Initiator
- Model, and
- Coach.

Initiator

Superior leaders **initiate** various actions and processes for building their work units into superior teams. The basic guideline for initiating team development is to make teamwork the norm for all actions. The way to initiate team development is to involve the team at the very outset in the process.

The Model for Superior Team Development and Performance provides a template for team-development actions. The model views team development and performance as the result more of a conscious decision by a work group to be a team than of the work group's tasks or the quality of the larger organizational environment. The model provides any work group with quite an array of alternatives for developing itself as a team and improving its performance. But nothing in the model has any practical utility unless the model is used by a work unit that is interested in becoming a superior work team. The model reflects what superior work teams look like and denotes what any team, group, or unit can do to become a superior work team.

Initiating team development is largely a process of setting goals. Goal setting has been shown to be the most consistently reliable strategy for influencing performance. Goal setting has an impact on the direction of a team's effort, on the strength of a team's effort, and on the duration or persistence of a team's effort (Locke et al. 1981). The more specific the goals, the more likely it is that teams will develop effective strategies for achieving them.

The initiator role of a team leader largely means that the leader helps bring the work group to make the following conscious decisions:

- to reaffirm in a clear, unambiguous way the intention to become or continue to improve as a superior work team;

- to set aside quality time to develop strategies and identify opportunities for significant improvement as a team;

- to determine what near- and long-term changes should be planned to ensure that the team is structured to continue to develop and function as a superior team; and

- to focus on the long-term future of the team and the kinds of knowledge and skills that the team must have to continue as a superior team.

Model

The team leader **models** the kinds of performance and behavior that serve to develop the team. In the simplest terms, this means that the team leader models what is expected of team members.

The fundamental characteristics of a superior work team that I have already identified in the Model for Superior Team Development and Performance are the very characteristics that I have found embodied in superior-work-team leaders.

Team leaders model team membership in two ways. First, they model it in the way they conduct their own business and perform their own tasks. Second, they model it in the way they interact with their colleagues.

Results. Team leaders model, for instance, the three subelements in the key element Results: making maximum use of human resources, achieving superior outputs against all odds, and showing continuous improvement. They are models by embodying the processes in themselves and in the way that they interact with the team.

Team leaders model the Result of making maximum use of a team's human resources in the way they are committed to using their own competencies and in developing new competencies. They are perceived as persons who are hard-working, curious, continuously learning, and actively seeking new opportunities to apply their competencies. They accept personal challenges and are seen as persons who are easily taught by others.

Team leaders also model what it means to make the maximum use of human resources in their interactions with others. They delegate easily and avoid micromanagement. They fully support the training of all team members and aggressively go after resources to support training. They help other team members cope positively with disappointments and failures. They ensure that other team members are involved in tasks that they feel are challenging and interesting.

These observations also pertain to the other Results—superior outputs against all odds, and continuous improvement. Superior-team-leaders model these results in what they personally achieve in taking action to ensure that the team achieves these results.

Informal Processes. Team leaders also model the Informal Processes in the Model for Superior Team Development and Performance: communicating and contacting, responding and adapting, influencing and improving, appreciating and celebrating. They model these

Processes both in their own behaviors and in the actions they take to ensure that the Processes are alive and well throughout the whole team.

Take, for example, communicating and contacting. Superior-work-team leaders model this Process in their own behavior by making frequent informal contact with other team members. They model good listening and problem-solving skills. They make it easy for others to be frank and open in the way they communicate. They are easily available.

They also model this Process in the actions they take to ensure that other team members communicate and stay in contact. They work at simplifying paper work because they know that paper is a barrier to personal contact. They hold regular team meetings.

What I have observed about communicating and contacting is true of the other three Informal Processes. Superior leaders model these processes in their own behavior and in the actions they take to ensure that the processes are functioning throughout the team.

Feelings. Superior team leaders know what it feels like to be a member of a superior work team. They model the behaviors that support the development of these feelings both in themselves and in others.

They nurture the sense of inclusion by a variety of actions. They ensure that

- they have balanced contact with all team members;
- team members get information that affects their jobs and their lives in the organization;
- the right team members attend the right meetings;
- team members are involved in making decisions that affect them;
- everyone's ideas are treated with respect;
- all team members have a fair chance at challenging work;
- appreciation is communicated to team members for their performance and value to the team;
- practical concern is shown for each team member's well-being;

- people have the chance to demonstrate their full competence; and

- there are frequent opportunities for team members to participate together in a variety of social events.

Coach

The third role that superior-work-team leaders frequently occupy is **Coach.** Coaching has emerged as a commonly accepted role for team leaders (Hackman and Walton 1986; Peters and Austin 1985; Semler 1989). From my studies of superior work teams it is apparent that Coach is a role that superior-work-team leaders frequently occupy.

I have treated the subject of coaching in detail in my book *Coaching for Commitment* (Kinlaw 1989), and I will not repeat that information here. What I will do is describe briefly what coaching is and outline its four major functions.

Coaching encompasses a multitude of informal conversations that a team leader has with individual team members or with groups of team members. In these conversations the leader carries out four distinguishable functions:

- counseling
- mentoring
- tutoring, and
- improving performance.

These four functions, all disciplined, problem-solving conversations, differ primarily in that they have different outcomes.

For example, when **counseling** the team leader is trying to achieve such outcomes as

- exploration of alternatives;
- accurate descriptions of problems and their causes;
- technical and organizational insight;
- venting of strong feelings;
- understanding some mandated change; and
- resolution of some confusion or misunderstanding.

Typical outcomes of **mentoring** are

- development of political savvy and sensitivity;
- Understanding the way an organization does business;
- building personal and team networks;
- insight and opportunities for team members to manage their careers;
- renewed commitment to the team's goals and values; and
- sensitivity to the values and biases of the people to whom the team must respond.

Typical outcomes from **tutoring** are

- increased technical competence;
- increased breadth of technical understanding;
- movement to an expert status;
- increased learning pace; and
- commitment to continuous learning.

Typical outcomes from **confronting** are

- clarification of performance expectations;
- identification of performance shortfalls;
- acceptance of more difficult and challenging tasks;
- strategies to improve performance; and
- commitment to continuous improvement.

The three roles that superior-work-team leaders frequently occupy are Initiator, Model and Coach. There are doubtless other roles and different ways to organize or classify them. I have focused on these three roles because they are clearly apparent in the behavior and performance of superior team leaders, and because they represent the roles that are most likely to be absent in the behavior and performance of team leaders who are not superior.

Summary

In this chapter I have discussed the final element in the Model for Superior Team Development and Performance, Leadership. The purposes of this discussion have been twofold:

- to discuss the special characteristics of leadership in superior work teams; and

- to describe the special leadership roles that exist in superior teams.

Special Characteristics of Superior-Work-Team Leadership

Special characteristics of Leadership in superior work teams include

- leading through teamwork; and

- always staying focused on both team development and team performance.

The practical meaning of leading through teamwork is that leaders of superior work teams emphasize:

- team performance more than individual performance; and

- commitment, not control, as the way to achieve superior performance.

The practical meaning of a leadership that is focused both on team development and on team performance is that leaders act on the knowledge that

- groups cannot perform at a superior level unless they have developed to a superior level; and

- developing the team must sometimes take precedence over everything else.

Superior Leadership Roles

The roles associated with superior leadership are:

- Initator
- Model
- Coach

The next chapter describes some Key Strategies that can be used to develop superior work teams.

8
Key Strategies for Superior-Work-Team Development and Performance

The Model for Superior Team Development and Performance has four primary elements:

- Results
- Informal Processes
- Feelings, and
- Leadership.

The fifth element in the model, Key Strategies, describes not characteristics of superior teams but what can be done to develop superior teams.

All five elements are displayed in the model to show that they are in continuous interaction with each other. At the center of the model are Key Strategies. These strategies are placed in the center of the interacting key elements and are called *Key* Strategies to emphasize

- that the model is an action model, intended to provide practical guidance for developing superior teams; and

- that although there are many ways to improve team development and team performance, these strategies have special relevance to the model.

In previous chapters, for each of the four primary elements in the model—Results, Informal Processes, Feelings, and Leadership—I have presented a number of strategic considerations. These strategic considerations are guidelines that can assist teams in considering alternative techniques and actions for developing their teams.

For example, when a team focuses on maximizing the use of its human resources (one of the key subelements of Results), it should remember that:

- the more competencies team members have a chance to use, the more competencies they will want to use—that is, competencies beget competencies;

- they can expand the development and use of competencies in an outward or horizontal direction;

- they can expand the development and use of competencies in a vertical or downward direction; and

- there are special team member competencies that must be developed and used.

In this chapter I will discuss the Key Strategies and how they can be used as formidable actions for improving a team's development and performance.

The Key Strategies

The Key Strategies have been selected with the following criteria in mind:

First, each strategy is clearly congruent with the model and targets one or more of the model's elements for improvement.

Second, the strategies typically have multiple impacts on team development and performance; that is, each strategy will tend to improve more than one of the model's primary elements or subelements.

Third, each strategy has been used in various seminars and team development projects and has proven merit.

Fourth, the strategies can only be used by teams. These strategies force teamwork. They have little or no value if used by individuals in some sort of unilateral action to improve their teams. *Teams can only improve through teamwork.*

Fifth, each strategy provides a clear conceptual basis for action. Each is in fact a descriptive model that has various elements that are clearly related.

Strategies are more comprehensive than techniques. They identify general targets, permit teams to identify a large number of specific targets and actions, and may employ many techniques like brainstorming, work simplification, or statistical process control.

The Key Strategies described in this chapter are:

- the model for Superior Team Development and Performance, used as a tool for planning for team development and performance;

- the Systems Model for Continuous Team improvement, used to insure that improvement is comprehensive and integrated;

- the Competencies and Influence Grid, used to ensure that a team is ensuring that team members are being fully utilized and are continuing to develop new competencies;

- the Team Meeting Effectiveness Model, used to help team members make the most of their planning and problem-solving meetings and to describe the kinds of skills required to make team meetings effective; and

- the Team Development Questionnaire, used to develop baseline data on the five Feelings associated with superior-work-team development.

Multiple Uses of the Key Strategies

Because of their special attributes, the Key Strategies have multiple uses. They can be used in at least six ways:

1. as analytical and assessment tools to identify team strengths and opportunities;

2. to educate team members about key issues in team development;

3. to devise very specific team-development actions;

4. to build baseline data for tracking team development and performance over time;

5. to develop common symbols and a common team vocabulary about development and performance; and

6. to communicate team-development actions and successes to outsiders.

Using the Model for Superior Team Development and Performance

The major and most comprehensive Key Strategy is the use of the Model for Superior Team Development and Performance (figure 3–2). The model provides the conceptual basis for understanding superior work teams and an outline for planning superior team development and performance. I suggest that the introduction of the model be among the first actions that teams take.

The model can be used in sequential steps.

First, the team reviews the model, four primary elements, and their subelements, then determines what meaning each element has for the team. The material in this book can provide the initial content for discussing the model. A recommended sequence to follow is:

1. One team member presents an overview of the Model.

2. Team members review in detail each of the elements and subelements and develop a common understanding of the elements.

Next, the team begins to build a plan for superior-work-team development by prioritizing the order in which they would like to address each element. Within each element, they then prioritize each subelement. The nominal group technique of weighted voting (see the appendix) can be used to develop the prioritized lists.

The team now has an outline of a logical and sequential plan for beginning its superior-team-development initiative. Specific actions have to be identified next. One help in identifying such actions is to review the remaining Key Strategies to determine how and when in the team's plan these strategies might best be used.

Using the Systems Model for Continuous Team Improvement

The Systems Model for Continuous Team Improvement (figure 4–3) is a model for any work unit that produces products or services for a customer, internal or external to the company. The systems model has the following elements:

- Suppliers—the individuals and groups who provide whatever it is that a team uses to perform its work and produce its output for some customer;

- Input—the forms, requests, materials, products, services, and the like that a team receives and on which it performs one or more operations to turn the input into output;

- Processes—all the sequential and parallel actions that a team takes to produce its output;

- Output—whatever leaves the team for use by some internal or external customer;

- Customer Forward Feed—information loop to anticipate customers' changing needs and requirements and to modify outputs and related processes;

- Customer Feedback—information loop to retrieve information about customers' satisfaction with current outputs and to determine requirements for new outputs and related processes;

- Supplier Forward Feed—information loop to help suppliers anticipate team members' or teams' changing needs and to change input and related processes;

- Supplier Feedback—information loop to keep supplier aware of team members' or teams' satisfaction with supplier input.

The positions of customer and supplier will sometimes be alternatively occupied by the same person or group. The personnel office, for example, is a customer of the training office when it requests training. The same office is, however, a supplier when it fills a staff vacancy in the training office.

The systems model helps teams to

- identify a wide variety of improvement opportunities; and

- consider how improvements in one element of the system relate to changes in other elements of the system.

A Wide Variety of Improvement Opportunities

The systems model helps in the easy identification of improvement opportunities. Take, for example, how a team in the business of providing training might use the model. Suppose the team chooses to focus on customer feedback. What strategies might the team employ to improve customer feedback? Here are a few alternatives:

- Conduct regular customer-satisfaction surveys.

- Conduct individual and group interviews with customers.

- Have customers compare the quality of the team's training programs with other, similar programs.

- Track all customer complaints; keep tracking updated, analyzed, and interpreted on a very regular basis.

Suppose the team wants to focus on its own internal processes. It might analyze any of the following processes:

- the process for designing new training programs;
- the process for producing training materials;
- the process of instructor preparation; and
- the process of participant accounting.

Or suppose the team focuses on its outputs. Examples of outputs might be identified as sales, customer service, and customer satisfaction. If the team decides to work on customer satisfaction, its strategies might be to

- guarantee all training programs to be 100 percent satisfactory and offer a full refund if requested;
- conduct extensive field tests of all new training programs before offering them;
- analyze reasons for success of any programs offered by competitors that are similar to what the team offers;
- provide customers with unlimited support as long as team's programs are used;
- guarantee delivery of all materials requested by customers within twenty-four hours.

The systems model helps teams raise questions about improvement in the following areas:

- improving the team's *Suppliers Feedback* Loop, to improve the services and products that it is provided
- improving the team's *Suppliers Forward Feed Loop,* to anticipate its new needs as they develop
- improving the team's *Processes,* used to transform its inputs and produce its outputs
- improving the team's *Customer Forward Feed Loop,* to anticipate its customers' changing needs and requirements and modify its processes accordingly
- improving the team's *Customer Feedback Loop,* to improve its customers' satisfaction.

The first function of the systems model is to stimulate teams to think of all the areas were improvement is possible. The second function of the model is to force teams to consider how an improvement in any one element of the systems model affects other elements.

Improvements in One Element of the System Affect Other Elements

A clear illustration of just how improvements can be interactive can be seen by looking at some work process. If the process of producing an output is improved, the output will be improved. Adding quality to the process will add quality to the product. If a team improves the quality of each sequential step in preparing, for example, travel vouchers, a higher and more consistent level of fitness for use will be obtained in the vouchers themselves. If a team can reduce the number of steps in filling a staff vacancy without reducing the quality of new hires, it has improved its output—that is, by filling vacancies in a briefer period of time.

Or suppose a team focuses on the inputs that it receives from its suppliers. If it is able to improve these inputs, it will improve its processes and ultimately its outputs.

Take again the example of filling a staff vacancy. If a team is able to receive more accurate information from the manager of a vacancy about the exact competencies of the person required to fill the vacancy, then its process for filling the vacancy becomes more error free and its output—the filled vacancy—has a higher quality.

The Systems Team Improvement Model is a very useful tool for discovering and planning improvement initiatives. First of all, it stimulates a work team to think of itself in its three roles of Supplier, Processor, and Customer and to consider the multitude of opportunities for improvement that result from these three roles. Second, the model helps teams to visualize the interrelatedness of any improvement initiative and to consider how an improvement in one element of the system might also improve other elements in the system.

Recommemded steps in using the Systems Team Improvement Model are:

1. The team reviews the model and each of its elements and talks through the meaning of each of the elements until all

members are clear about the information the model represents. This process can be initiated by one team member presenting an overview of the model.

2. The team prioritizes the order in order in which it would like to address each element. The nominal group technique of weighted voting (appendix) can be used to develop prioritized lists.

3. The team now has an outline of a logical and sequential plan for continuous improvement. Specific actions will, of course, have to be identified.

Using the Competencies and Influence Grid

The Competencies and Influence Grid (figure 4–2) provides the framework for evolving and selecting strategies to improve the use of people's competencies and to extend their influence. Using more of people's competencies and opening up new ways for them to be influential are clearly inseparable activities. Influencing and improving is one of the Informal Processes identified in the Model for Superior Team Development and Performance (figure 3–2).

The grid does not provide mutually exclusive cells; rather, there is considerable overlap among cells. The same examples of using competencies and influence may fit into more than one cell. The purpose of the grid is not to provide for a careful and exact cataloging of the competencies and influence used but to help team members identify what they now do and what they could begin to do.

The purpose for using the grid as a strategy for making maximum use of people is quite straightforward.

First, team members must decide whether they will use the grid to focus on competencies or influence. The use of team member's competencies and the degree of influence that team members are able to exert are both measures of the way a team makes use of its human resources. It is helpful, however, to clarify the way the grid will be used—to examine the use of comptetencies or the degree of influence.

Team members review the grid and make certain that all team

members understand it. The best way to test for understanding is to have team members provide a few examples for each of the cells in the grid.

Next, team members list as many current examples of how they use their competencies (or exert influence) in each of the grid's cells. Brainstorming can be used here quite beneficially.

Team members then list as many new opportunities for using their competencies (or exerting influence) that they can identify in each of the grid's cells. Brainstorming can also be used here quite beneficially.

In the next step, team members examine the two lists and determine where and how they should build new opportunities for team members to use their competencies (or exert influence).

The kinds of questions that use of the grid should prompt are:

- How much of their mental abilities can team members apply to the way they do their jobs? To the way the team functions? To the way the larger organization is run?

- Where do people have a chance just to give answers and input information, to talk about what they know? Is the information they have applied to the needs of their jobs? To the needs of the team? To the needs of the organization?

- Are people able to improve their jobs with their ideas? Are their ideas used to improve the team? To improve the larger organization?

- Where do people have the opportunity to make decisions? What can they decide about their jobs? The team? The larger organization?

- Are people fully utilized in solving problems that affect their jobs? The team? The larger organization?

If a team tries to identify only a single new strategy for each of the cells in the grid, the result would be twelve new strategies.

Using the Team Meeting Effectiveness Model

Team meetings are integral to the development of work units into superior work teams. Team meetings are required for the ongoing processes of sharing information and ideas, of setting goals, of making decisions, of solving problems, and of introducing and managing change. We can expect more and more that jobholders will be members of several teams at the same time. They will be members of their own permanent work team, but they will likely serve as members of a variety of temporary teams and special focus teams like productivity teams, interface teams, tiger teams, action teams, and the like. Team members require the skills to organize team meetings and to function as team members and leaders during team meetings.

It is unnecessary to give a detailed description of the various skills that are required to make team meetings effective and efficient. A number of useful books have already been published on this subject (Boreman and Boreman 1972; Bradford 1976). What is necessary is for teams to have practical model for understanding their team meetings and for ensuring that these meetings, like all other team activities, are positive factors in teams' ongoing development.

Effective and efficient team meetings result from the potential of the team and the performance of the team.

The *potential* of a team is composed of its assets—what it has before it begins a team meeting. The *performance* of a team is what it does with its potential—how it uses its potential in real time.

The potential of a team is made up of two elements: *resources* and *structure*. The performance of a team during a meeting is largely a function of how well its members *communicate*. Performance is the way the team communicates and makes use of its resources and structure.

The relationships between team meeting efficiency and effectiveness, potential and communication can be summarized as:

Efficiency and Effectiveness (f) Potential $(+)$ or $(-)$
Communication

Where the meaning of potential is:

Potential (f) Resources and Structure

Resources

Team resources that impact on team meeting effectiveness are:

- having clarity about the purpose of the team meeting and its value;
- having access to the information required to achieve the purposes of the meeting;
- having the facilities and equipment for the meeting;
- having the necessary quality time to conduct the meeting;
- having the financial resources to support team decisions; and
- having the right people at the meeting.

Structure

The second element in a team's potential to have an effective meeting is structure. How will the team meeting be organized to do its business during the meeting? Key elements in structuring a team meeting are:

Roles. Will there be a leader? What are special roles of each member? Is the role of the more senior members different from that of the more junior ones? Are there experts? What is the role of the boss? The more explicitly roles are identified and made evident to everyone, the better.

Norms. Norms refer to housekeeping rules. When will the team meet, start, and finish? Will it start on time and end on time? Will it start without everyone being present? Norms refer also to how the team will make its decisions. Will the team make decisions or only advise? Will decisions be made by consensus? By voting?

Norms refer, finally, to how the teams will interact. Is it an open, give-and-take interaction? Is open confrontation encouraged? How will conflict be managed? Is everyone responsible to insure that no one person monopolizes the team? The great value in taking time to establish clear and explicit norms is that the onus for enforcing timeliness, confronting people who tend to dominate, and managing other similar dysfunctional behavior is removed from any one person's responsibility. The team becomes responsible and reference to the norms becomes a way of managing the team.

Agenda/Goals/Objectives. What is the purpose of the team? What will it accomplish in the present meeting? What are the specific results that it is trying to achieve? It is useful to go beyond the typical agenda and identify what will result because a certain agenda item is covered.

Rational Process and Methods. The *rational process* is the sequence by which a team goes about achieving its task or objective. The important key action for a team is to make this process explicit. An example of a rational problem-solving sequence is:

1. Define the problem.

2. Develop a strategy for analyzing the problem.

3. Collect and analyze information.

4. Generate alternative solutions.

5. Evaluate and select a solution.

6. Plan action steps and accountability and measurement systems.

Within any given rational process, the team may employ a specific information-developing or problem-solving method. Typical of such methods are brainstorming, the nominal group technique, logical sequencing, and others. Here again, team effectiveness depends on the degree to which such methods are made explicit and the responsibilities of team members are clearly defined.

Team Meeting Evaluation. One of the most neglected subelements in structuring a team is team evaluation. Will the team evaluate its performance? If so, when and how?

Communication

One key to successful processes is how team members communicate. There are three elements in the communication process of a team.

Interpersonal Problem-Solving Processes and Skills. These are the processes and skills that are naturally present when information is mutually and easily developed. The first requisite for good team communication is that the team's members are able to interact in ways that help each other develop information, in ways that communicate respect, and in ways that develop positive relationships.

Task Achievement Skills. These are the skills that relate directly to the team's attempt to get on with its task. Examples of such skills are:

- Resourcing—giving information, proposing alternatives, suggesting procedures, and the like.

- Clarifying—interpreting ideas, clarifying confusion in a discussion, identifying common ground, and the like.

- Decision testing—checking for agreement, and testing to see if team is ready to make a decision.

- Summarizing—pulling together related ideas.

Group Process Skills. An effective team member helps the team remain conscious of how it is doing its business—how it is operating—through group process skills. Examples of team process skills are:

- Reminding the team of its norms, and letting the team know when it is keeping and not keeping its norms.

- Gate keeping—keeping communication channels open between members, and facilitating the participation of other members.

- Clarifying the rational or communication process—helping the team keep track of where it is as it follows some preplanned sequence, such as a problem-solving plan. Keeping the team conscious of breakdowns in the communication process, such as when members start interrupting each other and stop listening to each other.

Applying the Team Meeting Effectiveness Model

The Team Meeting Effectiveness Model can be applied in various ways. First, it is a very useful way for a team to educate itself on the general conditions for making its team meetings as effective as possible.

Second, the model can provide guidance for training a team in the specific skills that it needs for managing the team's resources, for structuring the team, and for communicating during a meeting.

Finally, the model can be used to establish norms and to evaluate a team's performance during meetings.

Using the Team Development Questionnaire

The Team Development Questionnaire (TDQ), found in the appendix a, assesses the Feelings element in the Superior Team Development Model. This section provides background information about the TDQ and describes the steps for using it as a team development strategy.

The purposes of the Team Development Questionnaire are to provide work group leaders and members with information about the level of team development within their work group; and to help work group leaders and members identify specific opportunities to improve team performance in their groups.

The TDQ is a fifty-item instrument that measures the self-reports of how strongly team members experience five Feelings that predict the level of team development in a work group. The more positive work-team members are about all these characteristics, the higher the level of team development in the group. The five Feelings are

- inclusion
- commitment
- loyalty
- pride, and
- trust.

Sample score sheets for the TDQ are included in appendix A. These sheets are used to analyze TDQ scores. There is a *sum* score in column 2 for each of the five variables. These scores identify the major strengths, weaknesses, and opportunities for the team.

- Characteristics that have average sum scores of 39 or over are *strengths* and are associated with high-performing teams and organizations.

- Characteristics that have average sum scores of 29 and less are *weaknesses* and are associated with poorly-performing teams and organizations.

- Scores that are between 30 and 38 are associated with average-performing teams and organizations and should be considered possible *opportunities* for improvement.

Summary

In this chapter I have reviewed several Key Strategies for developing superior work teams. These startegies are:

- The Model for Superior Team Development and Performance, used as a tool for planning for team development and performance;

- the Systems Model for Continuous Team Improvement, used to insure that improvement is comprehensive and integrated;

- the Competencies and Influence Grid, used to ensure that a team is ensuring that team members are being fully utilized and are continuing to develop new competencies;

- the Team Meeting Effectiveness Model, to help team members make the most of their planning and problem-solving meetings and to describe the kinds of skills required to make team meetings effective; and

- the Team Development Questionnaire, used to develop baseline data on the five Feelings associated with superior-work-team development.

Conclusion

I began this book by observing that there are two realities that are shaping organizational life in America today. The first reality is that many organizations are under serious pressure to improve their performance in order to gain a competitive position and to survive. The second reality is that the most consistently successful strategy to improve performance has proven to be the use of teams and teamwork.

It is not, however, just the development of teams and the use of teamwork that will produce the required high level of quality in services and products. Superior performance is also required, and superior performance is only possible through superior teams.

My work with a variety of organizations has shown me that managers and other key people have a serious commitment to teamwork and team development. What they do not have is a practical model that they can use to develop their teams for superior performance. I have set out in this book to provide such a model. The information I have provided can be particularly useful for people involved in the business of planning and implementing TQM.

I have intended this book to be of practical use

- as a self-help guide for leaders to make their work groups into superior work teams;

- as a conceptual basis for trainers to use to equip others to build superior work teams;

- as an adjunct resource for participants involved in any team-development program; and

- as a special guide for people having responsibilities in TQM team-development initiatives.

The book has been organized around presenting the Model for Superior Team Development and Performance, a model derived from my own experience as a consultant and from my studies of work teams. The model reflects several conclusions about superior work teams:

First, superior work teams produce Results that are quantitatively and qualitatively different from other work units. These results include

- maximum use of a team's human resources;
- superior outputs against all odds; and
- continuous improvement.

Second, superior work teams use distinctive, day-to-day Informal Processes like

- communicating and contacting;
- responding and adapting;
- influencing and improving; and
- appreciating and celebrating.

Third, superior-work-team members have the persistent positive Feelings of:

- inclusion
- commitment
- loyalty
- pride, and
- trust.

Fourth, superior work teams develop Leadership that is focused on both development and performance. Superior Leadership has quite special orientations.

• It is always oriented toward the team and teamwork.

• It is always oriented toward both team development and team performance.

Superior leaders also perform the special roles of:

• Initiator
• Model, and
• Coach.

Fifth, a set of Key Strategies fully support superior-work-team development and can be used to plan, organize, and implement a comprehensive program of superior-work-team development.

Most of the material in this book has been devoted to describing and explaining the Model for Superior Team Development and Performance. But a number of other models that I have developed over the years and found very useful tools for instruction and team development are also presented. These tools are:

• Work Group Task Flows (figure 1–1);

• Relationships of Work Groups, Work Teams, and Superior Work Teams (figure 1–2);

• Distinctions between Team Building and Team Development (figure 2–1);

• Relationship of Team Building to Team Development Actions (figure 2–2);

• Arenas for Improving the Use of People (figure 4–1);

• The Competencies and Influence Grid (figure 4–2);

• The Systems Model for Continuous Team Improvement (figure 4–3); and

• Influence Process and Payoffs (figure 5–1).

I can think of no better way to end a book on superior work teams than to describe one to which I was quite recently introduced.

I first met this team during a TQM seminar that I led. I learned a good bit about the team during the seminar, and I have made a point of finding out even more since.

The team is an air-compressor shop of an East Coast engineering firm. The shop has eight members, and all except the supervisor are members of a union. The ages of the shop's members range from late twenties to early fifties.

This team has gotten so many cash awards through the company's suggestion program that some of the rules in the suggestion system have had to be rewritten. In the past two years, one member alone has received over $35,000.

After finishing the TQM seminar, this team invited the company's productivity manager and CEO to come to its shop on a Friday afternoon to hear what improvement projects it had planned during the seminar.

The members that I have had a chance to interview in some depth describe just how great it is to go to work. They talk about actually missing the job and the people when they aren't at work and of never having had a bad day. As impossible as it may sound, I believe that each of the members of this team are always "up," always happy in their jobs, and somewhat outrageous in the way they think about themselves. Over and over again, one after another of them has said to me that they have "the best team of its kind," that they are "the best team in the company," and "they wouldn't trade jobs with anybody." These remarks are made by the younger members of the team as well as the older ones. There is absolutely no evidence of distinctions made because of age. The older men go out of their way to tell me just how bright and valuable the younger members were. The younger members volunteered to tell me how much they continued to learn from the older members.

The team's admiration of their supervisor is so positive that I have felt a bit self-conscious at times listening to the members. "He is the best there is." "I have worked with him for five years, and we have never once even had a cross word." "There ain't nobody around who can do what he can do."

One member puts his experience on the team in perspective by describing his experience in two companies prior to his present job.

This is the first time that I have had a chance to think. Mr. ———, our top man, came down when this team was put together and told us he expected us to think and that we were getting paid to think. He told us that if we could do anything better or make any kinds of improvements, then do it. Where I used to work, we were treated like kids. We could never start a job unless our supervisor told us to. And every single detail was laid out. You had to go ahead and do a job, even when you knew it was being done wrong and that you would have to come back an do it over. If you wanted your butt kicked, just do anything at all that you weren't told to.

What ticked me off was that everything was so political. You got the jobs to do because of how well the supervisor liked you. And overtime was passed out the same way. I hated my job. I used to feel physically sick a lot. But now, it's the difference between night and day. This is the greatest company in the world, and I work with greatest bunch of guys in the world. Now I've got only one problem and that is dealing with the people who are just plain jealous of us and our reputation.

One senior manager confided to me that his biggest problem is trying to enforce a few controls just to keep this team from creating too many problems with other people who have turfs to protect.

This is a union shop, remember. These guys have a habit of putting their other union buddies on notice. They will tell the painters and maintenance people for instance, "We want this or that painted by such and such a date, and if you don't do it, we will do it ourselves." They do so much more than most other teams because they just won't let the formal system stop them. And they are able to get away with it most of the time because they have done so many favors for so many people that everyone owes them and they just keep calling in their chips.

Superior work teams are the single comprehensive answer to improved performance. They are a proven strategy for ensuring quality in services and products. They certainly provide the solution to gaining a competitive edge in the marketplace. Superior work teams, however, are also much more. As it turns out, superior work teams provide people with work environments where they have the best chance to be fulfilled and happy in their work.

Appendix: Tools for Improving Team Development and Performance

Brainstorming

Brainstorming is a group technique for generating information by the spontaneous contribution of ideas from all group members. Typically, the steps are:

1. Clarify the ground rules for brainstorming.

2. Define the topic or information target.

3. Go around to each member of the group initially and request ideas in sequence.

4. Record all ideas.

5. End with input in any order from members.

6. Follow these rules in generating ideas:

   - one idea at a time
   - allow no criticism or discussion
   - record all ideas, even if they seem repetitious
   - piggyback on ideas

7. Review all the ideas and clarify them. Do not eliminate them, only reword them as needed.

8. Review all the ideas, and combine the ideas that are redundant.

9. Review, clarify, and make additions to develop a final list of ideas.

The Nominal Group Technique

The Nominal Group Technique (NGT) is a highly structured brainstorming approach to information generation and problem solving. NGT employs a series of sequential steps:

1. a clear definition of the problem or objective of the session;

2. the independent generation of ideas and information by group members;

3. a sequential and objective listing of ideas and information from group members;

4. a discussion and clarification of listed items;

5. a preliminary vote on item importance; and

6. a final vote.

NGT requires the use of a facilitator. Facilitating the NGT process is not difficult, but it does require clear knowledge of the process and some practice. Facilitators cannot participate as members of the group using NGT because they have a full-time job managing the NGT process. Facilitators may be drawn from group members, or they may be external to the group. The role of facilitator can also be rotated between group members. But however facilitators are selected, *the role of the facilitator is critical to the success of NGT.*

Step 1: Definition of the Problem or Objective

NGT focuses the group on a specific problem, question, or objective, such as:

- What are the obstacles for improving productivity in our work group?
- What can we do to increase most dramatically the productivity in our team or organization?
- How can we measure the quality of our products?

These definitions of the problem are written down as a statement.

Step 2: Individual Generation of Ideas

The question or problem statement is displayed so the whole group has a clear view of it. Each member records his or her own responses to the question.

Cards may be used to record ideas, one idea per card. The cards are collected.

Step 3: Sequential Listing of the Ideas

The facilitator records the ideas of the group by listing them on a flip chart. The facilitator lists one idea in turn from each card. If cards have not been used, the facilitator asks each member in turn for one idea at a time.

This way of generating and recording ideas eliminates several problems that are sometimes associated with problem-solving group sessions, such as fear of criticism, conservative involvement, hidden agendas, and the like.

Step 4: Discussion and Clarification

All the items are reviewed, and obvious duplications are removed. Only duplicate items are removed from the list. Items are then clarified. The potential usefulness of items is not discussed.

Step 5: Preliminary Vote

Preliminary voting is done in a way that avoids influences and pressures of status, personality, and conformity. It can be done in a variety of ways; the process described here employs cards.

The facilitator distributes an appropriate number of cards to each member, who are then asked to review the list of ideas and select the items—equivalent to the number of cards they have—that are most important for resolving the identified problem or responding to the question.

In the upper left-hand corner of the card, the members put the number of the item, corresponding to its number on the flip chart. In the center of the card, they write the complete description of the item as it appears on the chart.

Members then review the items and select from their cards the one that is best. They place in the lower righthand corner the number equivalent to the total number of cards. If eight cards are used, then the number is eight.

Members select the card with the item that is least important or useful for the problem at hand, and place the number 1 in the lower righthand corner. They evaluate all the remaining cards in this least-best pattern.

The facilitator collects the cards and posts the results. The preliminary vote is discussed to identify any strong disagreements and to insure that everyone has the same information and understanding.

Step 6: Final Vote

A final vote is taken (if it is necessary to reduce the list further). The same procedure can be followed as that used in step 5, or various weighting techniques can be used.

Team Development Questionnaire*

The Team Development Questionnaire (TDQ) is based on studies conducted by the author, Dr. Dennis C. Kinlaw, and studies of other researchers, in which the characteristics of superior teamwork

---

and superior work teams were studied. The TDQ has been designed to:

1. Give work-team members a tool to assess their work teams and to compare the results to the key characteristics of superior work teams;

2. Help work-team members identify specific targets to improve their teams' development;

3. Provide leaders in organizations (when data from work teams are summarized) with a profile of the total organization's level of team development.

Directions

The TDQ can be used to assess the level of team development in the following kinds of teams.

- Permanent Work Team. This is the team of people with whom you daily work and who have a specific organizational name. For example, this team may be a branch, a section, a long-term project team, a management team, or a manager and staff.

- Temporary Team. This is a team of people who have been joined together for a specific short-term task. They usually represent a variety of organizations. Examples are quality circles, special project teams, performance improvement teams, accident investigation teams, tiger teams, and the like.

- Interface Team. This is a team made up of two or more teams from different organizations that have a permanent work relationship and that must cooperate to get their jobs done. Examples are interfaces between users and contractors, design and manufacturing and marketing, operations and maintenance, electrical and mechanical subsystems, procurement and users, training and users, and the like.

In completing the TDQ you must be consistent about the "work team" you are rating. Follow the steps below and complete the TDQ.

1. Indicate the company or organization to which you belong, e.g., Grumman Technical Services, NASA Kennedy Space Center, EG&G, etc., and the date on which you are completing the TDQ.

   Company/Organization _____ Date _____

2. Name the work team on which you are completing the TDQ and give the team's mail code (if it has one).

   Work Team _____ Mail Code _____

3. Each item in the TDQ presents a characteristic that may describe your work team to some degree or that may not describe your work team at all. Indicate the degree to which you believe the item accurately describes your own work team by circling the appropriate number on the scale (5 to 1) that appears with each item. "5" indicates that you completely agree. "1" indicates that you do not agree at all.

4. Complete *every* item.

5. Return your completed TDQ to the person or address designated and by the date indicated on the special directions you have received.

In my team:	Completely Agree				Completely Disagree
1. My input is taken seriously when the team sets priorities.	5	4	3	2	1
2. I am regularly consulted before changes are made that affect me.	5	4	3	2	1
3. There are no cliques that create devisiveness.	5	4	3	2	1
4. We make sure that members are properly acknowledged for their performance.	5	4	3	2	1
5. We celebrate the successes of					

our whole team as much as we do the successes of individual team members.	5	4	3	2	1
6. People with the less glamorous jobs are shown as much appreciation as those with the more glamorous jobs.	5	4	3	2	1
7. The team members who are closest to a problem typically get the first shot at fixing it.	5	4	3	2	1
8. We pay a lot more attention to what our members know than we do to their rank or position.	5	4	3	2	1
9. We typically get all the information we need to do our best work.	5	4	3	2	1
10. We treat every team member's ideas as having potential value.	5	4	3	2	1
11. I am quite clear about my team's major goals.	5	4	3	2	1
12. We are all fully committed to building our team into the best one possible.	5	4	3	2	1
13. I am quite clear about our team's immediate priorities.	5	4	3	2	1
14. We are all committed to the highest possible standards of quality in everything we deliver for someone else to use.	5	4	3	2	1
15. Team members rarely let their personal feelings get in the way of getting the job done.	5	4	3	2	1
16. Our team members rarely					

work by the clock; they do
what's necessary to do the job
right.   5   4   3   2   1

17. When we face a problem,
    everyone jumps in and works
    until it's resolved.   5   4   3   2   1

18. We all believe that what we
    are doing is truly important.   5   4   3   2   1

19. Our team members often
    make significant personal
    sacrifices to insure the team's
    success.   5   4   3   2   1

20. Our team members are
    typically optimistic that we
    can get the job done—
    regardless of the obstacles.   5   4   3   2   1

21. It's easy to get help from
    other team members, when I
    need it.   5   4   3   2   1

22. We go out of our way to
    ensure the success of our
    fellow team members.   5   4   3   2   1

23. I never hear one team
    member criticizing another
    team member to a third party.   5   4   3   2   1

24. We spend a lot more time
    praising the work of team
    members than we do finding
    fault with it.   5   4   3   2   1

25. When one team member has
    a personal problem and
    wants help, he/she can count
    on help from other team
    members.   5   4   3   2   1

26. We never surprise a team
    member in public with
    comments that might
    embarrass the member.   5   4   3   2   1

27. When any team member can't carry his/her share of the workload, other team members will always jump in and take up the slack.   5   4   3   2   1
28. We regularly help each other to learn new competencies.   5   4   3   2   1
29. When we do get into conflicts, we typically resolve them right away.   5   4   3   2   1
30. We never take credit for someone else's work.   5   4   3   2   1
31. We pride ourselves on doing a job better than most people typically expect.   5   4   3   2   1
32. We never make excuses if anything our team does isn't right.   5   4   3   2   1
33. Our members feel strongly that everything our team does represents each member personally.   5   4   3   2   1
34. We expect that we will completely satisfy our customers and users (within and outside the company).   5   4   3   2   1
35. I derive a great deal of personal satisfaction from being a part of our team.   5   4   3   2   1
36. Team members typically take any criticism of our team as a possible opportunity to improve.   5   4   3   2   1
37. We are our own most severe critics.   5   4   3   2   1
38. We know exactly how well we are doing at all times.   5   4   3   2   1
39. I am very clear how our team

contributes to the total success of the organization.	5	4	3	2	1
40. We are typically very positive to others about our team's performance.	5	4	3	2	1
41. When a team member says he/she will do something, you can always count on it.	5	4	3	2	1
42. My fellow team members typically give me information that is 100 percent accurate.	5	4	3	2	1
43. When team members don't know something, they will always tell you they don't and not act like they do.	5	4	3	2	1
44. When a team member doesn't agree with another team member, he/she will let the other member know— regardless of the other member's position or rank.	5	4	3	2	1
45. Our team members always keep sensitive team business within the team.	5	4	3	2	1
46. Our team members typically demonstrate the highest form of personal honesty and integrity.	5	4	3	2	1
47. Team members rarely conceal anything from another member that they feel the member should know.	5	4	3	2	1
48. When a member gives the team bad news, we never "shoot the messenger."	5	4	3	2	1
49. Our team members always assume that there are very					

good reasons if any member fails to fulfill a commitment.	5	4	3	2	1
50. You can get a straight answer from anyone about anything you want to know.	5	4	3	2	1

Team Development Questionnaire Score Sheet

Team: _____ **Date:** _____

1 Item	2 Team Average	3 Individual Ratings									4 Range
		A	B	C	D	E	F	G	H	I	
1											
2											
3											
4											
5											
6											
7											
8											
9											
10											
Char. Average											

TDQ Characteristic: Inclusion

1 Item	2 Team Average	3 Individual Ratings									4 Range
		A	B	C	D	E	F	G	H	I	
11											
12											
13											
14											
15											
16											
17											
18											
19											
20											
Char. Average											

TDQ Characteristic: Commitment

1 Item	2 Team Average	3 Individual Ratings									4 Range
		A	B	C	D	E	F	G	H	I	
21											
22											
23											
24											
25											
26											
27											
28											
29											
30											
Char. Average											

TDQ Characteristic: Loyalty

1 Item	2 Team Average	3 Individual Ratings									4 Range
		A	B	C	D	E	F	G	H	I	
31											
32											
33											
34											
35											
36											
37											
38											
39											
40											
Char. Average											

TDQ Characteristic: Pride

1 Item	2 Team Average	3 Individual Ratings									4 Range
		A	B	C	D	E	F	G	H	I	
41											
42											
43											
44											
45											
46											
47											
48											
49											
50											
Char. Average											

TDQ Characteristic: Trust

References

Aviation Week and Space Technology. 1988 (January 8): 62.

Boreman, E.G., and N.C. Boreman. 1972. *Effective Small Group Communication.* Minneapolis, Minnesota: Burgess.

Bradford, L.P. 1976. *Group Development.* San Diego: University Associates.

Briggs, G.E., and W.A. Johnston. 1967. *Team Training* (Technical report #1327-4). Orlando, Florida: Naval Device Training Center.

Bulker, P.F. 1986. "Effects of Team Building and Goal Setting on Productivity: A Field Experiment." *Academy of Management Journal* 29 (no. 2): 305–328.

Business Week. 1981. "The New Industrial Relations." (May 11): 84–98.

Business Week. 1989. "The Payoff from Teamwork." (July 10): 56–62.

Davis, J.A. 1969. *Group Performance.* Reading, Massachusetts: Addison-Wesley.

Dyer, W.G. 1977. *Team Building: Issues and Alternatives.* Reading, Massachusetts: Addison-Wesley.

Hackman, J.R. 1978. "The Design of Work in the 1980s." *Organizational Dynamics* (Summer): 3–17.

Hackman, J.R. 1983. *A Normative Model of Work Team Effectiveness* (Technical report #2). Research Program on Group Effectiveness, Yale School of Organization and Management. Arlington, Virginia: Office of Naval Research.

Hackman, J.R., E.E. Lawler, III, and L.W. Porter, eds. 1977. *Perspectives on Behavior in Organizations.* New York: McGraw-Hill.

Hackman, J.R., and C.G. Morris. 1975. "Group Tasks, Group Interaction Processes, and Group Performance Effectiveness: A Review and Proposed Integration." In L. Berkowitz, ed., *Advances in Experimental Social Psychology,* vol. 8. New York: Academic Press.

Hackman, J.R., and G.R. Oldman. 1980. *Work Design.* Reading, Massachusetts: Addison-Wesley.

Hackman, J.R., and R.E. Walton. 1986. "Leading Groups in Organizations." In P.S. Goodman, ed., *Designing Effective Work Groups*. San Francisco: Jossey-Bass.

Holpp, L. 1989. "10 Reasons Why Total Quality is Less than Total." *Training* (October): 93–103.

Kinlaw, D.C. 1990. *Coaching Skills Training*. San Diego: University Associates.

Kinlaw, D.C. 1989. *Coaching for Commitment*. San Diego: University Associates.

Kinlaw, D.C. 1983. "Getting Motivated Employees to Perform." *Supervisory Management* (October): 10–14.

Kinlaw, D.C. 1981. *Listening and Responding*. San Diego: University Associates.

Klein, J.A. 1984. "Why Supervisors Resist Employee Involvement." *Harvard Business Review* (September/October): 87–95.

Kolodny, H., and M. Kiggundu. 1980. "Towards the Development of a Sociotechnical Systems Model in Woodlands Mechanical Harvesting." *Human Relations* 33: 623–645.

Kondo, Y. 1988. "Quality in Japan." In J.M. Juran and F.M. Gryna, eds., *Juran's Quality Control Handbook*. New York: McGraw-Hill.

Lawler, E., III. 1986. *High Involvement Management*. San Francisco: Jossey-Bass.

Locke, E.A., K.N. Shaw, L.M. Saari, and G.P. Latham. 1981. "Goal Setting and Task Performance." *Psychological Bulletin* 90: 125–152.

McDonnell, D. 1989. "Organizational Changes Evolve through TQM." *Focus* 3 (May 11): 1–2.

Miller, L. 1984. "Tearing Down the Barriers between Management and Labor Leads to Increased Productivity and Greater Profits." *Management Review* (May): 8–15.

NASA Excellence Award for Quality and Productivity: Application Guidelines 1989–1990. 1989. Washington, D.C.: NASA.

Nieva, V.F., E.A. Fleishman, and A. Rieck. 1985. *Team Dimensions: Their Identity, Their Measurement, and Their Relationships*. Alexandria, Virginia: U.S. Army Research Institute for the Behavioral and Social Sciences.

Nora, J., C.R. Rogers, and R. Stramy. 1985. *Transforming the Work Place*. Princeton, New Jersey: Princeton Research Press.

Peters, T. 1989. *Thriving on Chaos*. New York: Harper & Row.

Peters, T., and N. Austin. 1985. *A Passion for Excellence: The Leadership Difference*. New York: Random House.

Peters, T., and R. H. Waterman. 1982. *In Search of Excellence: Lessons from America's Best Run Companies*. New York: Warner Books.

Quality and Productivity Improvement: 1988 Accomplishments Report. 1989. Washington, D.C.: NASA.

Reich, R.B. 1987. "Entrepreneurship Reconsidered: The Team as Hero." *Harvard Business Review* (May/June): 77–83.

Scherkenbach, W.W. 1988. *The Deming Route to Quality and Productivity.* Washington, D.C.: CeePress Books.

Semler, R. 1989. "Managing Without Managers." *Harvard Business Review* (September/October): 76–84.

Sherwood, J.J. 1988. "Creating Work Cultures with a Competitive Advantage." *Organizational Dynamics* (Winter): 5–27.

Steiner, I.D. 1972. *Group Process and Productivity.* New York: Academic Press.

Stogdill, R.M. 1981. *Stogdill's Handbook of Leadership,* revised by B.M. Bass. New York: Free Press.

Techknowledge. 1989. "AT&T Vendors on a Quality Team." (October): 10.

Techknowledge. 1989. "Baldridge Competition Keeps Suppliers Competitive." (October): 3.

Thamhain, H.J., and D.L. Wilemon. 1987. "Building High Performing Engineering Project Teams." *IEEE Transactions on Engineering Management* 34 (no. 3, August): 130–137.

TQM Message. 1989. (September): 1. Washington, D.C.: Department of Defense.

Varney, G.H. 1989. *Building Productive Teams.* San Francisco: Jossey-Bass.

Wagner, H., N. Hibbits, R. Rosenblatt, and T. Schulz. 1977. *Team Training and Evaluation Strategies: State of the Art* (Technical report #77-1). Washington, D.C.: HUMRO.

Weist, W.M., L.W. Porter, and E.E. Ghiselli. 1961. "Relationship between Individual Proficiency and Team Performance and Proficiency." 45:435–440.

Werther, W.B. 1981. "Productivity Improvement through People." *Arizona Business* (February): 14–19.

Yankelovich, D., and J. Immerwahr. 1983. *Putting the Work Ethic to Work.* New York: The Public Agenda Foundation.

Recommended Additional Reading

Bales, B. M. 1950. *Interaction Process Analysis: A Method for the Study of Small Groups.* Reading, Massachusetts: Addison-Wesley.

Belbin, R. M. 1981. *Management Teams: Why They Succeed or Fail.* London: Heinemann.

Cummings, T. G. 1978. "Self-Regulating Work Groups: A Socio-Technical Synthesis." *Academy of Management Review.* 3: 625—634.

Cummings, T. G. 1981. "Designing Effective Work Groups." In P. C. Nystrom, and W. H. Starbuck, eds., *Handbook of Organizational Design,* vol. 2. London: Oxford University Press.

Davis, J. A. 1969. *Group Performance.* Reading, Massachusetts: Addison-Wesley.

Gladstein, D. 1984. "Groups in Context: A Model of Task Effectiveness." *Administrative Science Quarterly* 29 (no. 4): 499–517.

Faust, W. L. 1959. "Group Versus Individual Problem-Solving." Journal of Abnormal and Social Psychology 59: 68–72.

Fayne, R., and C. L. Cooper, eds. 1981. *Groups at Work.* Chichester, United Kingdom: Wiley.

Hare, A. P. 1972. "Bibliography of Small Group Research." *Sociometry* 72: 1–150.

Hare, A. P. 1976. *Handbook of Small Group Research,* 2nd ed. New York: Free Press.

Hastings, C. 1986. *The Superteam Solution: Successful Teamworking in Organizations.* Aldershot, England: Gower.

Howe, R. J. 1977. "Building Teams for Increased Productivity." *Personnel Journal* (January): 16–22.

Janis, I. L. 1982. *Groupthink,* 2nd ed. Boston: Houghton Mifflin.

Jewell, L. N., and H. J. Ritz. 1981. *Group Effectiveness in Organizations.* Glenview, Illinois: Scott, Foresman & Co.

Kinlaw, D. C. 1988. "What Employees 'See' Is What Organizations Get." *Management Solutions* (March): 38–43.

Klein, J. A. 1984. "Why Supervisors Resist Employee Involvement." *Harvard Business Review* (September/October): 87–95.

Lawler, E. E., III, and S. A. Mohrman. 1985. "Quality Circles after the Fad." *Harvard Business Review* (January/February): 65–71.

McGrath, J. E. 1984. *Groups: Interaction and Performance.* Englewood Cliffs, New Jersey: Prentice-Hall.

McGrath, J. E., and I. Altman. 1966. *Small Group Research: A Synthesis and Critique of the Field.* New York: Holt, Rinehart, and Winston.

Merry, U., and M. E. Allerhand. 1977. *Developing Teams and Organizations.* Reading, Massachusetts: Addison-Wesley.

Miles, M. B. 1981. *Learning to Work in Groups,* 2nd ed. New York: Teachers College Press.

Morris, C. G. 1966. "Task Effects on Group Interaction." *Journal of Personality and Social Psychology.* 5: 545–554.

Schultz, W. C. 1955. "What Makes Groups Productive?" *Human Relations* 8:429–465.

Shaw, M. E. 1971. *Group Dynamics: the Psychology of Small Group Behavior.* New York: McGraw-Hill.

Shaw, M. E., and P. Caron. 1965. "Group Effectiveness as a Function of the Group's Knowledge of Member Dissatisfaction." *Psychonomic Science* 2: 299–300.

Sorenson, J. R. 1971. "Task Demands, Group Interaction, and Group Performance." *Sociometry* 34: 483–495.

Woodcock, M., and D. Francis. 1981. *Organization Development through Teambuilding.* Aldershot, England: Gower.

Woodman, R. W., and J. J. Sherwood. 1980. "The Role of Team Development in Organizational Effectiveness: A Critical Review." *Psychological Bulletin* 88: 166–186.

Index

About the Author

Dennis C. Kinlaw, Ed.D., has been a consultant in organizational development and management education for over twenty years. He is currently president of his own consulting company, Developmental Products, Inc., in Norfolk, Virginia, which specializes in team development and total quality management.

Dr. Kinlaw received his doctorate in adult education from The George Washington University. He has taught graduate courses for The American University, The George Washington University, and Virginia Commonwealth University in the areas of management theory and practice, and adult learning.

He has authored numerous articles in management and training journals and has conducted original studies in management behavior, leadership, interpersonal communication, and team performance. He is also the author of the book entitled *Coaching and Commitment* and has written various video-assisted training programs and individual and organizational assessment instruments.

Dr. Kinlaw has consulted with over fifty public and private organizations and has been a principal consultant to NASA for the past fifteen years. He received NASA's Special Service Award in 1986 for his work in performance measurement and productivity.

DATE DUE			
DEC 09 '93			
FEB 06 '95			
OCT 16 '95			
NOV 2 1 2007			